Travel Guide To

Girona,
SPAIN

Escape to Spain: Your Go-To Resource for an Amazing Trip!

Wybikes Hinton

COPYRIGHT NOTICE

DISCLAIMER

Please note that the information contained within this document is for educational purposes only. The information contained herein has been obtained from sources believed to be reliable at the time of publication. The opinions expressed herein are subject to change without notice.

Readers acknowledge that the Author / Publisher is not engaging in rendering legal, financial or professional advice. The Publisher / Author disclaims all warranties as to the accuracy, completeness, or adequacy of such information.

The Publisher assumes no liability for errors, omissions, or inadequacies in the information contained herein or from the interpretations thereof. The publisher / Author specifically disclaims any liability from the use or application of the information contained herein or from the interpretations thereof.

TABLE OF CONTENT

Contents

Copyright Notice ii
Disclaimer iii
Table of Content iv
Introduction 1
Introduction to Girona! 1

Why Girona? A Brief Overview 2

How to Get to Girona: Flights, Trains, and Road 2

When to Visit Girona in Different Seasons 3

Girona's History: A Journey Across Time 4

Girona Essentials: Language, Currency, and Safety Tips 5

Chapter 1 7
Getting Around Girona 7

Public Transportation: Buses and Taxis 7

Biking in Girona: A Cyclist's Dream 9

Walking Tours: Exploring by Foot 10

Car Rental and Parking Tips 12

Navigating Girona: Maps and GPS Applications 13

Chapter 2 15
Girona's Old Town (Barri Vell) 15

Historic Walls: Passeig de la Muralla 16

Jewish Quarter (Call Jueu): A Cultural Treasure 17

Girona Cathedral: A City Symbol 18

Plaça de la Independència, Girona's Heart 19

Arab Baths: A Glance into Medieval Architecture 21

Chapter 3 23
The Game of Thrones Experience in Girona 23

Key Filming Locations Near Girona 24

Guided Tours of the Game of Thrones sets 26

Interesting Facts From Behind the Scenes 27

The Cathedral Stairs: A Memorable Moment 28

Exploring the King's Landing Experience 29

Chapter 4 31
Culinary Delights of Girona 31

Girona's Best Restaurants: Michelin Star Dining 32

Food Markets: Mercat del Lleó 34

Best Cafes and Coffee Shops in Girona 36

Girona's Wine & Craft Beer Scene 37

Cooking Classes: Learn Local Recipes 38

Chapter 5 40
Art and Culture in Girona 40

The Museum of Art in Girona: Artistic Heritage 41

Contemporary Art Spaces and Galleries 42

Girona's Festivals: Schedule Your Visit for Events 43

Street Art in Girona: Hidden Gems 45

Girona Cultural Performances: Theaters and Shows 46

Music in Girona: Classical, Jazz, and Modern 47

Chapter 6 50
Shopping in Girona 50

Best Shopping Streets and Areas 51

Souvenirs to Take Home: Locally Made Items 52

Girona's Boutiques: Clothing and Accessories...........53

Specialty Shops: Cheese, Olive Oil, and More 54

Antique Stores and Flea Markets...........56

Shopping Malls and Department Stores...........57

Chapter 7 59
Day Trips from Girona 59

Costa Brava: Exploring the Mediterranean Coast...........60

Banyoles Lake: A Relaxing Getaway...........61

Figueres and Dalí Museum 62

La Garrotxa: Hiking in the Volcanic Region...........63

Pals and Peratallada: Medieval Villages...........65

Montserrat Monastery: A Spiritual Escape...........66

Chapter 8 68
Outdoor Adventures in Girona 68

Hiking trails in Girona...........69

Kayaking in the River Ter 70

Cycling Routes: Girona's Cycling Legacy 71

Hot Air Balloon Rides Over The City...........72

Rock Climbing and Adventure Sports 73

Birdwatching at Girona's Wetlands 74

Horseback Riding Tours: Scenic Rides...........75

Chapter 9 77
Girona's Parks and Gardens...........77

Parc de la Devesa, Girona's Green Heart...........78

Jardins dels Alemanys: A Garden of History 79

Parc del Migdia: Relax and Unwind 80

Montjuïc Castle & Gardens 81

River Walks Along The Onyar....................................82

Botanical Gardens Around Girona 83

Chapter 10...85
Girona by Night 85

Best Bars and Nightclubs in Girona..........................86

Evening Strolls and Romantic Spots..........................87

Night Tours of Girona's Landmarks...........................89

Live Music Venues for a Fun Night............................90

Best Places for Late-Night Snacks 91

Nightlife Etiquette in Girona 92

Chapter 11...94
Festivals and Events in Girona 94

Temps de Flors, Girona's Flower Festival...................95

Girona's Sant Narcís Fair 96

Film Festivals and Cultural Week 98

Sporting Events and Marathons 99

Music Festivals & Concerts 100

Seasonal Markets and Craft Fairs 101

Chapter 12...103
Family-Friendly Activities in Girona.........................103

Best Places to Visit With Kids.................................104

Girona's Child-Friendly Museums 105

Parks and Playgrounds for Families 106

Day Trips Suitable for Children 108

Girona Waterparks and Aquatic Activities...............109

Family-Friendly Restaurants and Cafés..................................111

Chapter 13...113
Religious and Spiritual Sites of Girona......................113

Girona Cathedral: A Majestic Symbol 114

Saint Pere de Galligants Monastery..............................115

Església de Sant Feliu: Girona's Oldest Church 116

Sant Daniel Monastery: Peace and Serenity...................117

Jewish Heritage Sites and Synagogues 118

Religious Festivals and Traditions 119

Chapter 14..122
Accommodation in Girona 122

Overview of Accommodation Options............................123

Luxury Hotels and Resorts 124

Mid-range Hotels for Comfort 125

Unique Stays 126

Staying Near Girona's Old Town 127

Boutique Guesthouses...128

Top Recommended Hotels and Resorts..........................129

Choosing the Right Accommodation for You...................130

Booking Tips to Get the Best Deals 131

Chapter 15..133
Health and Wellness in Girona 133

Spa and Wellness Centers..134

Yoga Retreats and Meditation Spots 135

Gyms and Fitness Centers in Girona 137

Girona's Outdoor Wellness Activities 138

Where to Find Medical Help and Pharmacies 139

Health Tips for Travelers in Girona 140

Chapter 16... 142
What to Do and Not Do in Girona 142

Cultural Etiquette: Respect for Local Customs 143

Tourist Tips: How to Behave Like a Local..................................145

Common Mistakes to Avoid as a Tourist 146

Safety Tips for Travelers...147

Environmental Awareness: Green Travel 149

Legal Regulations: What You Should Know 150

Chapter 17... 152
Girona's River Onyar 152

Girona Bridges: Iconic Structures...153

Colorful Houses Along the Onyar...154

River Walks: Scenic Trails 155

Photography Locations along the River 157

Riverside Cafés and Restaurants...158

Water Activities at Onyar..159

Chapter 18... 161
Off the Beaten Path Girona 161

Hidden Gems: Lesser-Known Attractions 162

Secret Streets in the Old Town 163

Explore Girona's Lesser-Known Neighborhoods......................165

Unique Museums and Galleries...166

Girona's Best Kept Local Secrets...167

Chapter 19...170
Sustainable and Environmentally Friendly Travel in
Girona 170

Environmentally Friendly Hotels and Accommodations..........171

Sustainable Restaurants and Cafes...........................173

How to Travel Green in Girona 174

Supporting Local Businesses and Communities.....................175

Reduce Your Carbon Footprint While Traveling 176

Responsible Wildlife Watching and Tours 178

Chapter 20...180
Girona's Local Markets 180

Mercat del Lleó: Girona's Main Market 181

Street Markets and Seasonal Events 182

Best Places to Buy Local Produce...184

Farmers' Markets Around Girona 185

Food Tasting and Sampling in Markets.....................................186

Chapter 21...189
Girona for Returning Visitors 189

Rediscovering Girona: New Experiences 190

Updates and Recent Developments in the City 191

Hidden Gems for Experienced Travellers..................................193

Advanced Tours and Specialized Itineraries 194

Reconnecting with the Girona Locals 195

Chapter 22...198
Unique Itineraries & Sample Plans 198

A Three-Day Itinerary for First-Time Visitors.........................199

A Week in Girona: Exploring beyond the Surface....................201

Girona and Costa Brava: A Combined Trip Plan.......................203

A Four-Day Foodie Tour of Girona 204

A Cycling Tour Itinerary for Girona 205

A Game of Thrones Fan's Two-Day Itinerary 206

A Relaxation and Wellness Retreat Plan...................................207

Chapter 23.. 209
Conclusion and Final Thoughts 209

Reflecting on Girona's Unique Charm.......................................210

Make the Most of Your Time in the City....................................211

Must-See Spots Before You Leave 212

Final Travel Tips for the Perfect Trip...213

A Warm Farewell from Girona...215

Chapter 24.. 216
Useful resources... 216

Emergency Contacts 217

Maps and Navigation Tools..218

Additional Reading and References..220

Useful Local Phrases 221

Glossary..222

Addresses and Locations for Popular Accommodation 224

Addresses and Locations of Popular Restaurants and Cafés ...225

Addresses and Locations of Popular Bars and Clubs 227

Addresses and Locations of the Top Attractions 228

Introduction

INTRODUCTION TO GIRONA!

If you have never been to Girona before, you are in for a big treat. Girona, located in northeastern Spain, is one of those hidden gems that does not draw attention to itself, but once you arrive, you'll wonder why you waited so long to visit. It's the ideal blend of history, charm, culture, and modern flair, and it caters to all types of travelers. Girona has it all, whether you want to wander through historic neighborhoods, relax by the river, or eat delicious food.

Let me walk you through the essentials. After spending more time in Girona than I'd like to admit, I can tell you what makes it so wonderful. Buckle up, because once you've read this, you'll be booking your flights right away.

Why Girona? A Brief Overview

Imagine a place where you may walk along centuries-old city walls, get lost in narrow cobblestone lanes, and still have access to all of the amenities of a modern, bustling metropolis. That is Girona. It's tiny enough to explore on foot (without the need for a compass or a sherpa), yet vast enough to keep you busy. The first time I visited here, I was astonished by its diversity. One minute you're walking through medieval alleyways, the next you're enjoying a cortado at a stylish café overlooking the colorful residences along the River Onyar.

Girona has a knack of combining its ancient past with a modern air that seems refreshingly honest. It's not attempting to be Barcelona or Madrid, which is exactly the point. Girona's unique attractiveness stems from its simplicity. You won't find an Eiffel Tower or a Big Ben here, but you will discover a city full of understated beauty, delicious food, and a laid-back pace of life that feels like a warm hug after the hustle of more tourist-heavy cities.

How to Get to Girona: Flights, Trains, and Road

Getting to Girona is easier than you would expect. If you're traveling, you have two options: Girona-Costa

Brava Airport and Barcelona's El Prat Airport. Girona's airport is small, yet functional, and only 12 kilometers from the city center. El Prat in Barcelona is around 100 kilometers away, and from there, it's a short rail ride to Girona. And let me tell you something: if you enjoy staring out the window and wondering about your next tapas stop, the train ride is well worth it.

Speaking of trains, Girona is well connected by Spain's high-speed AVE trains, which travel from Barcelona in around 40 minutes. I've found this to be the most convenient mode of transportation—plus, there's something wonderful about arriving in a city via rail. You can also drive to Girona, but be prepared for small streets and parking that demands the skills of a Formula One driver. The roads are picturesque, weaving through Catalonia's lush landscapes, so a small road trip is a possibility.

When to Visit Girona in Different Seasons

Girona is one of those places where each season brings something special. I visited in the spring, summer, and fall, and each time it felt like I was discovering a new city. Let me break it down.

- Spring (March-May): Girona's world-renowned flower festival, Temps de Flors, takes over the entire city in May. Imagine every street, garden, and balcony bursting with bright blooms. It's as if Mother Nature's

Instagram account had blossomed in the finest way conceivable. If you enjoy mild weather and less crowds, spring is the best season to visit. Plus, did I mention the flowers?

- Summer (June–August): It gets warm. Very warm. But if you can stand the heat, summer in Girona promises exciting festivals, outdoor music, and relaxing afternoons by the river. The old city's stone walls appear to trap the heat, but get some gelato and you'll be fine. One perk? Longer days allow you more time to explore, and the Mediterranean beaches are only a short drive away.

- Fall (September–November): My particular favorite. The summer throngs have dispersed, the temperature has cooled, and Girona's fall festivals begin. Also, it's wine season! There's something about walking through Girona's autumn-kissed streets with a glass of local wine in hand that makes you feel like you've discovered a hidden gem of Spain.

- Winter (December-February): Although it is chilly, winter in Girona is charming. The festive lights are turned on, the cafes create a warm ambiance, and the city becomes quieter and more intimate. In addition, if you enjoy skiing, the surrounding Pyrenees are ideal for a fast getaway. No crowds, no rush—just you and Girona at its most tranquil.

Girona's History: A Journey Across Time

Girona proudly displays its history, and if you're anything like me, you'll fall in love with its medieval beauty. The city is nearly 2,000 years old, with layers of history heaped on top of one another. Walking through the old town feels like you've traveled back in time. There is Roman history, medieval fortifications, and Europe's best-preserved Jewish Quarter.

Let's start with the Roman walls, officially known as the Passeig de la Muralla. You may walk around these old fortifications and see panoramic views of the entire city. It's one of those times that makes you realize how little you are in the larger scheme of history. The walls themselves date from the first century BC and were expanded during the medieval period. So, yes, you are walking on some big history.

Then there's the Jewish Quarter, also known as Call Jueu. Girona was home to a strong Jewish community from the ninth to the fifteenth centuries, and the twisting, narrow alleyways still bear witness to that history. I've been through the Jewish Quarter innumerable times, and each time I discover something new—a hidden courtyard, a stone-carved Star of David, or simply a moment of quiet thought in its winding alleys.

Girona Essentials: Language, Currency, and Safety Tips

Let's get practical—because, while getting lost in Girona's beauty is wonderful, you'll also need to know how to get around.

First up: language. Girona is in Catalonia, thus while most people speak Spanish, you'll also hear Catalan, which is a distinct language from Spanish. Don't worry if your Spanish isn't perfect; most residents speak English, especially in tourist regions. However, mastering a few fundamental Catalan phrases will help you enchant the locals. I always like to add a casual "Bon dia!"" (Good morning!) just to watch their eyes brighten up.

In terms of currency, we are in the Eurozone, thus you will be using the Euro. ATMs are widely available, and most locations accept credit cards, but have some cash on hand for smaller shops or markets. Tipping is not expected, however rounding up the amount or leaving a few Euros for good service is appreciated.

Finally, safety. Girona is extremely safe, but employ common sense like you would anywhere else. Pickpocketing isn't a big deal, but keep a check on your belongings, especially in crowded situations or festivals. I've never felt unsafe in Girona, including at night, although it's always a good idea to be mindful of your surroundings.

And there you have it: the fundamentals for getting started in Girona. Believe me, this city will sneak up on you in the greatest manner possible.

Chapter 1

GETTING AROUND GIRONA

Getting around Girona is one of the best parts of visiting this city. It's a place that's small enough to explore on foot or by bike while also huge enough to offer something new every day. Unlike some larger European towns, where you may spend hours negotiating maze-like subway systems or waiting for a bus that never appears, Girona is surprisingly straightforward to get around. Here's how I got around while in Girona, and how you can, too.

Public Transportation: Buses and Taxis

To be honest, when I initially arrived in Girona, I had lofty plans to walk everywhere and only take buses and cabs when necessary. That lasted almost two days. While Girona is a lovely walking city, you'll want to rest your feet every now and then, especially when the midday heat makes you feel like you've walked directly into a pizza oven. So, let's talk about the unsung heroes of Girona transportation: buses and taxis.

Girona's bus network is efficient, inexpensive, and easy to use. TMG (Transports Metropolitans de Girona) operates the city's buses, which travel across the city to both popular tourist destinations and more local, off-the-beaten-path communities. I discovered that buses were especially useful when I wanted to travel further out, such as to Parc de la Devesa, a big green park on the outskirts of town where you can picnic beneath the shadow of towering trees. The buses are frequent, typically clean, and, most significantly, air-conditioned—an essential feature if you travel during the summer. Tickets can be purchased at kiosks, but if you plan on taking the buses frequently, you can obtain a T10 card, which grants you 10 rides at a reduced rate. It's a lifesaver, especially when you're moving across town.

Now for taxis. There are several of them in Girona, and you may hail one from almost anywhere in the city or find one at official taxi ranks. They're metered, so no bartering is required (thank goodness), and they're especially convenient when you're laden with bags after a day of shopping or returning late from one of Girona's wonderful restaurants or pubs. My personal advise is to write down the name of your destination in Spanish or Catalan (particularly if it's a lesser-known location), as not all drivers speak English. I once asked a driver to take me to "Plaça de la Independència," but the look on his face suggested that I was asking to go to a distant planet. Lesson learned!

Biking in Girona: A Cyclist's Dream

Girona is a cycling heaven. Now, I'm not a professional cyclist—I'll leave the Tour de France dreams to the Lycra-clad riders who pass by—but even a casual rider like myself couldn't help but note how bike-friendly Girona is. Biking in Girona is a dream not only because of the beautiful scenery and moderate Mediterranean climate, but also because the city appears to be designed specifically for cycling.

The first thing you'll notice is the overwhelming amount of bicycle shops scattered around the city. Girona is a destination for professional cyclists, with many of them training here throughout the offseason. On any given day, you'll find groups of bikers cruising up into the hills surrounding the city, taking on the twisty roads that snake through the countryside. There's something almost poetic about the image of bikers silhouetted against the backdrop of the Pyrenees, peddling with ease as if gravity were a suggestion.

But don't worry if you're a more slow biker, like myself. Girona is flat in many locations, making it ideal for leisure biking. I rented a bike from one of the town's many bike shops, and the staff was polite, full of information on the best routes, and didn't laugh (at least not too hard) when I inquired if the bike included training wheels. The River Onyar is one of Girona's top cycling routes. The trail is smooth, picturesque, and largely traffic-free, so you can enjoy the splendor of Girona without having to dodge cars.

Another must-do is riding up to Els Àngels, a local mountain with a chapel located on top. It's a bit of a climb, but the panoramic vistas at the summit are worth every drop of sweat. For those who are less motivated to defy gravity, there are flatter routes, such as the Vies Verdes, a network of former railway lines turned bicycle trails that wind through the Catalan countryside. Whether you're a serious cyclist or just enjoy pedaling at a moderate pace, Girona is a two-wheeled adventurer's paradise.

Walking Tours: Exploring by Foot

Girona is a walkers' paradise. I could go on for hours about how walking in Girona is like meandering through a storybook. You don't need a car, a bike, or even a map (although we'll cover that later). You only need a pair of comfortable shoes. The city is meant to be explored on foot, and every turn seems to bring a new discovery—whether it's a hidden courtyard, a beautiful café, or a centuries-old archway that appears to have appeared out of nowhere.

The Old Town (Barri Vell) is where I spent the majority of my time walking aimlessly. And that's the key to enjoying Girona on foot: don't plan too much. Sure, keep a few essential places in mind, such as Girona Cathedral (which you'll recognize as a Game of Thrones filming location) or the Jewish Quarter, but allow plenty of time to get lost. Believe me, getting lost in Girona is a luxury.

Walking around the Passeig de la Muralla, the city's ancient walls, made me feel like a character from a history novel. You are raised above the city, with panoramic views of Girona's terracotta rooftops, distant mountains, and the twisting River Onyar. It's not a tough walk, but it's long enough to get away from the noise and bustle of the city. Along the journey, you'll come across vantage points and towers that are ideal for capturing photos or simply enjoying the scenery.

Let us not forget about Girona's bridges. The Pont de Pedra and the Pont de les Peixateries Velles are two prominent bridges that straddle the River Onyar and provide breathtaking views of the colorful buildings that border its banks. I found myself crossing these bridges several times a day, constantly pausing to enjoy the scenery. It's the kind of view that never grows old.

If you're like me, you'll want to participate in one of Girona's guided walking tours. They're guided by local guides who know the city like the back of their hand,

and they're packed with fascinating facts you wouldn't have learned otherwise. Did you know that Girona has been besieged 25 times in its history? Or that the Girona Cathedral has the world's largest Gothic nave? Walking tours are an excellent opportunity to learn about the city's history, architecture, and culture while also getting your daily steps in.

Car Rental and Parking Tips

Let us chat about driving in Girona. Or, more specifically, let's discuss whether you should even bother driving in Girona. Here's my take: don't. Driving in Girona is more pain than it's worth, unless you intend to take day trips outside of the city. The streets are tiny and generally one-way, and navigating them is like to playing Tetris with vehicles as the pieces. Additionally, there is the issue of parking.

During one of my trips to Girona, I rented a car since I thought it would be the most convenient way to see the surrounding countryside. It was, but when it came to parking in the city, I quickly realized I had taken on more than I could handle. Parking in the Old Town is essentially non-existent, unless you have a time machine that can transfer you back to a medieval era when parking places did not exist. Parking is a challenge in the city's newer neighborhoods. Most street parking is metered, and getting a spot during peak hours is like winning the lottery—possible, but unlikely.

However, if you are determined to drive, there are a few parking garages throughout the city. Parking Saba Santa Caterina is one of the more central and handy options, but it fills up rapidly, particularly on weekends. My advice? Use it as a last resort, and only if you intend to stay in the city for a limited time. Otherwise, park the car at your hotel or Airbnb and explore the city on foot or by bike.

If you rent a car, I recommend taking day trips to the Costa Brava or the Pyrenees, both of which are fairly accessible from Girona. Just make sure to ask your car rental company about local traffic rules (and whether your insurance covers narrow medieval streets—kidding, sort of).

Navigating Girona: Maps and GPS Applications

Despite Girona's small size, it's easy to get lost, especially in the network of streets that make up the Old Town. This is where maps and GPS applications come in handy. Even though I like to think of myself as having a good sense of direction, there were several occasions when I found myself in a street that didn't appear on any map. But that's part of Girona's appeal—getting lost is like a rite of passage.

For the practical traveler, there are numerous options for navigating the city. Google Maps is, of course, a reliable resource. It's wonderful for pinpointing particular locations and providing walking directions, but in the Old Town, the meandering lanes might be confusing. Maps.me was another tool I used frequently, particularly when I needed offline map access (quite useful if you want to avoid data charges). This software allows you to download maps ahead of time and shows additional information of minor streets and alleys.

If you prefer a more traditional approach, many tourist offices and hotels provide complimentary paper maps. They're simple but helpful for gaining an overview of the city's layout. And, let's be honest, there's something nostalgic about unfolding a paper map, drawing your path with your finger, and then refolding it into a crumpled mess that never quite fits back into your bag.

Getting around Girona is a pleasure, whether you take the bus, taxi, bike, or walk. Every means of transportation has its own charm, and each one provides a unique perspective on this fascinating city. Every moment feels like an adventure, whether you're speeding down the river-side cycling trails or strolling aimlessly through the ancient streets of Old Town. Just remember to pause, look around, and breathe it all in, whether you're walking or driving. Because that is the enchantment of Girona: it urges you to slow down, explore, and relish every step (or pedal) of your journey.

Chapter 2

GIRONA'S OLD TOWN (BARRI VELL)

Stepping inside Girona's Old Town, or Barri Vell, feels like crossing a time barrier, where the past and present coexist in wonderfully imperfect harmony. This portion of the city, with its cobblestone alleys, high medieval walls, and secret corners, is what makes Girona memorable long after you've left. It's a place where history isn't just something you read about in books; it's beneath your feet, in the walls around you, and lingering in the air as you walk through narrow alleys that have been around for hundreds of years.

Allow me to lead you around some of the most fascinating portions of Barri Vell, where every corner tells a story and every stone appears to speak its own mysteries.

Historic Walls: Passeig de la Muralla

If you, like me, enjoy panoramic vistas (and a little exercise), the Passeig de la Murallais is the place to begin your investigation of Girona's old town. The traditional walls that surround much of the old city date from Roman times, but they were enlarged during the medieval period. Walking over the top of these walls provides some of the best views in the city, and they are nothing short of breathtaking.

Consider going down a stone road that snakes around the city, providing panoramic views of Girona's orange-tiled rooftops, the shimmering River Onyar, and the verdant hills beyond. It's the kind of view that makes you want to stop every five steps and take another photo—and believe me, I did. The walls itself feel ancient and imposing, with towers and lookout points that make you imagine what it must have been like to be a guard gazing over the city centuries ago.

One of my favorite sections of the hike was the Torre Gironella, a tower that appears to be as old as time. Climbing to the top of this tower provides an even better perspective, and it's worth every intake of breath as you make your way up the stone steps. Make sure to bring a bottle of water, especially if you're working on the walls during the warmer months. You'll thank me later when you're standing at the top, gazing out over Girona with the breeze in your face, feeling like a conqueror surveying their realm.

The nicest feature about the Passeig de la Murallais is that it is free to use and can be accessed from many spots throughout the city. Whether you complete the entire loop or simply a piece, it's a must-see for anybody visiting Girona. It's also one of the few activities where you can burn off the calories from all the tapas you'll undoubtedly consume without feeling like you're working out.

Jewish Quarter (Call Jueu): A Cultural Treasure

Walking around Girona's Jewish Quarter, or Call Jueu, is like exploring a living museum. It's one of Europe's best-preserved Jewish districts, with a maze of narrow, winding lanes that seem locked in time. You'll find yourself slipping beneath archways, peering into little courtyards, and feeling as if you've stumbled onto a hidden world that few people get to see.

The Call Jueudates dates back to the Middle Ages, when Girona had a strong Jewish community that contributed much to the city's culture and business. Walking around this neighborhood, it's difficult not to imagine the stories these streets could tell—the families who lived here, the intellectuals who studied in its synagogues, and the tragic periods that eventually led to Jews' exile from Spain in 1492. This portion of the city has a weight to it, a sense of history that lingers in the air like a heavy fog.

One of the Call Jueu features is the Museum of Jewish History, which is built in a former synagogue. It's a small museum, but it's jam-packed with fascinating relics and displays that provide insight into the daily life of Girona's medieval Jewish community. I spent more time here than I expected, captivated by the stories of persistence, faith, and cultural interaction that built this section of Girona. In addition, if you're visiting during the heat, the museum is a terrific location to cool off—just saying.

Take your time while wandering through the Jewish Quarter. These streets are made to be explored leisurely, with numerous excursions down small alleys that lead to hidden jewels. One of my favorite finds was a tiny patio hidden beneath an ordinary stone bridge. There was a single olive tree in the center, and for a moment, I felt as if I had the entire city to myself.

Girona Cathedral: A City Symbol

If Girona had a crown jewel, it would surely be Girona Cathedral. You can't miss it, literally. The cathedral dominates the skyline, and its huge stone steps are among the most memorable images of the city.

But the Girona Cathedral is more than simply a beautiful backdrop for your Instagram account. It represents the city's strength and spirit, having survived sieges, battles, and centuries of wear and tear. The cathedral's most striking feature is its nave, which is the widest Gothic nave in the world. When you step inside, the sheer size of the place takes your breath away. Even though I'm not especially religious, standing in that immense, echoing room made me feel awed.

The cathedral's exterior is a detailed masterwork of Baroque design, with figures and carvings that appear to come to life as the sun travels across the sky. And then there's the ascent. Yes, the 90-odd stone steps are steep, but the view from the summit is well worth the effort. Not only do you get a close-up look at the exterior, but the views over the Old Town are breathtaking.

The Tapestry of Creation is a centerpiece inside. This 11th-century embroidered tapestry is a medieval art masterwork that depicts episodes from the Bible and world history. It's one of those things that you have to see to believe—photos can't capture the incredible detail and artistry that went into its production.

Visiting Girona Cathedral is one of those must-see events that no vacation to the city is complete without. Just be prepared for weary legs afterwards—those steps are no joke.

Plaça de la Independència, Girona's Heart

Every city has a heart, a location where life appears to beat a little faster, where locals and tourists alike come to unwind, interact, and watch the world go by. Plaça de la Independència is the name of that location in Girona. This vast, open area is flanked by exquisite neoclassical buildings and lined with cafés and restaurants that spill out onto the sidewalks, tempting you to sit down, order a coffee or a glass of wine, and soak it all in.

Throughout my stay in Girona, I found myself returning to Plaça de la Independència several times, generally for a coffee break in between viewing the city's ancient attractions. Something about the square makes it an ideal location for people-watching. Locals rush by on their way to work, children play by the fountains, while visitors like myself sit with maps in hand, plotting our next excursion.

The area is called after the War of Spanish Independence, and a massive monument in the center commemorates the city's resistance to Napoleon's army. Despite its historical significance, Plaça de la Independència is far from a depressing location. It's bright, dynamic, and full of energy— especially in the evenings, when restaurants are packed with people enjoying long dinners and lively conversation.

If you're looking for somewhere to dine in Girona, this is the place. There are plenty of excellent restaurants here, serving everything from traditional Catalan delicacies to cosmopolitan cuisine. One evening, I chose to indulge in escudella i carn d'olla, a hearty Catalan stew, followed by crème catalana for dessert. Let's just say that I had no regrets.

Arab Baths: A Glance into Medieval Architecture

Girona's Arab Baths, or Banys Àrabs, are a vestige of the city's medieval past, providing a peek into a time when public baths were a vital part of daily life. The name is somewhat misleading—these baths are not Arab, but rather designed in the Romanesque style, which was inspired by older Muslim bathhouses. Regardless of their origins, they are fascinating places to explore and offer a calm reprieve from the city's hustle and bustle.

The baths date back to the 12th century, and as you go through the numerous chambers, you can practically hear the echoes of the past—the splashing of water, the hushed talks, the sense of togetherness that these spaces must have created. The frigidarium (cold room) is the most striking feature of the complex, with its stunning domed roof supported by slender columns. The light coming in through the little windows provides a peaceful, almost ethereal environment.

While the baths are no longer in use, they are amazingly well-preserved, and going through the chambers gives you a sense of what it must have been like to visit them when they were most popular. It's one of those places where you enjoy the little joys of life, such as a nice bath after a long day of wandering through Girona's mountainous streets.

The Arab Baths are a quick but worthwhile stop on your tour of the Old Town. It's the type of spot where you can sense history all around you, and it serves as a reminder that Girona has been influenced over time by a variety of cultures and influences.

Exploring Girona's Old Town is like peeling back the layers of history, with each street, building, and monument providing a new view into the city's rich history. Barri Vell has a way of capturing you and making you feel like you've stepped into a different world, whether you're walking along the ancient walls, wandering through the Jewish Quarter, climbing the steps of the Girona Cathedral, relaxing in Plaça de la Independència, or exploring the quiet chambers of the Arab Baths. It's the type of location that remains with you long after you leave, and I guarantee that once you've been there, you'll be planning your next visit.

It's the type of location that stays with you long after you've left, and I guarantee that once you've been there, you'll be planning your next visit.

Chapter 3

THE GAME OF THRONES
EXPERIENCE IN GIRONA

I'll let you in on a little secret: I wasn't a Game of Thrones superfan before visiting Girona. Sure, I'd watched a few episodes, knew about the dragons, and even had a general idea of who sat on the Iron Throne (for a while). But my expertise didn't extend much beyond that. Then I arrived in Girona, and like a wildfire raging through Westeros, I was swept up in the Game of Thrones frenzy that pervades this stunning city. As it turns out, several crucial sequences from the show were filmed exactly here, and once you start exploring, you can't help but feel like you've landed in the Seven Kingdoms.

Girona may be a city steeped in ancient history, but it's also renowned to Game of Thrones fans as one of the real-world locations for King's Landing, Braavos, and Oldtown. Whether you're a die-hard fan or a casual viewer, the Game of Thrones experience in Girona is one of those unique travel highlights that you can't help but geek out about. Allow me to take you on a tour of the important filming locations, guided tours, and some interesting behind-the-scenes details that will make your stay in Girona feel like a voyage through Westeros.

Key Filming Locations Near Girona

You know those moments when you're going down the street and suddenly realize you've seen something before—on TV, in a movie, or even in a dream? That's precisely what happened to me in Girona. The city's narrow, cobblestone alleyways, high stone walls, and historic architecture provided the ideal setting for some of Game of Thrones' most memorable sequences. And once you recognize these areas, it's difficult to avoid thinking about dragons, sword fights, and, perhaps, the occasional betrayal.

One of the first places I came across was the Cathedral of Girona, well known as the Great Sept of Baelor among Game of Thrones enthusiasts. Remember the thrilling confrontation between Queen Margaery Tyrell and Cersei Lannister? That was filmed right here, on the great stone stairs leading to the cathedral. Climbing those steps feels like a rite of passage for any tourist to Girona—except, happily, there's no chance of wildfire. The first time I stood at the foot of the steps, I half expected to see a group of armed guards marching down, but instead I was welcomed by a few other tourists uncomfortably reenacting their favorite scenes (don't worry, I'm guilty of the same).

Another important site is the Basilica of Sant Feliu, which you may remember as one of the streets of Braavos. If you remember Arya Stark's quest to becoming a Faceless Man, you'll recall her traversing the streets of Braavos, begging and training. Some of the scenes were perfectly suited to the Basilica of Sant Feliu. The gothic architecture and meandering lanes surrounding the basilica are obviously medieval, and it's easy to envision Arya hiding in the dark, planning her next move.

Plaça dels Jurats, a calm area that has been transformed into Braavos' outdoor theatre, where Arya attends a play about the Lannisters, was one of my favorites. In real life, it's a quiet setting, ideal for sitting on a bench and reflecting—or reenacting Arya's knife fight, if that's more your style. Arya's chase sequences in Braavos were filmed in Carrer del Bisbe Josep Cartaña, a lovely street. Walking through these streets, it's clear to see why the Game of Thrones production chose Girona—the city already looks like it belongs in Westeros.

Guided Tours of the Game of Thrones sets

You could easily tour Girona's streets with a smartphone and Google, looking for filming sites, but what's the fun in that? The best way to completely immerse yourself in the Game of Thrones experience is to take a guided tour led by educated locals who can not only point you significant filming locations but also tell you some juicy behind-the-scenes anecdotes.

I joined up for one of these tours, and let me tell you, it was like entering into a completely different world—Westeros, to be specific. Our guide, a Girona local who had served as an extra on the show, was full of energy and insider knowledge from the moment we met. He shared a lot of interesting information about how the production team changed Girona into various regions of the Game of Thrones realm. For example, did you know that they employed CGI to make the Cathedral of Girona appear taller and more imposing? Or that some of the extras in the crowd sequences were Girona residents who spent a few days pretending to be people of King's Landing?

One of the highlights of the visit was the chance to examine side-by-side images of the real locales and their Game of Thrones counterparts. It's astonishing how much of Girona's natural beauty was included into the presentation with only a few digital tweaks. Plus, our guide told us a lot of funny stories about the filming process, like how a scene had to be reshot because a stray dog wandered into the frame, unaware that it was walking through the streets of Braavos.

The tour also included visits to local shops and eateries that had embraced their Game of Thrones-themed identity. Let's just say that the "Mother of Dragons" cocktail I enjoyed later was one of the highlights of the day.

Interesting Facts From Behind the Scenes

While exploring Girona's Game of Thrones sites, I discovered that creating a fantasy series on this magnitude is far more complicated (and funny) than you might expect. Sure, everything appears to be smooth and majestic on screen, but there were plenty of bloopers, technical difficulties, and, of course, stories about what it's actually like to film a hit TV show in a small medieval city.

For example, the Great Sept of Baelorsteps at Girona church may appear to be constructed for spectacular entrances, but during filming, the crew struggled to navigate the tight streets surrounding the church with their big equipment. There is one story about a camera crew attempting to catch the perfect sweeping image of the area, only to have a local street vendor unintentionally set up their stall exactly in the heart of the shot. The merchant refused to relocate, resulting in a confrontation reminiscent of a Game of Thrones scene.

Another fun fact: do you remember the famous moment in Braavos where Arya Stark jumps off a balcony and into a wagon full of oranges? That balcony is on Carrer de l'Escola Pia, and while it appears that Arya accomplished a death-defying performance, the actual fall was considerably more controlled. The production team constructed a platform and employed sophisticated camera work to make it appear as if she were free-falling. So much for Arya being a real superhero!

If you're a die-hard fan, you'll enjoy hearing how the production team converted Girona's modern characteristics into something more appropriate for Westeros. Many of the footage recorded in Plaça dels Jurats, for example, necessitated meticulous editing to substitute modern signage with medieval banners and flags. It's the little touches that make all the difference, and Girona's commitment to realism is what made her become such a convincing member of the Game of Thrones world.

The Cathedral Stairs: A Memorable Moment

Let us now discuss one of Girona's most recognizable places for Game of Thrones fans: the Cathedral stairs. These aren't ordinary stairs. These are the stairs where Cersei Lannister performed her notorious walk of atonement (though, to be fair, the real walk was filmed in Dubrovnik—but don't let that spoil the fun). However, the Girona Cathedral plays a significant role in Game of Thrones, appearing in a number of crucial moments.

There's something about standing at the bottom of those stone steps and gazing up at the Girona Cathedral that feels different when you see it on TV. It is one of those rare occasions when fantasy and reality clash in the most dramatic way possible. I attempted to go up the steps dramatically, thinking myself as one of Westeros' aristocratic families on their way to the Great September. In truth, it was a slow trek because the steps were steep, and let's just say I'm not cut out for medieval architecture.

The Cathedral stairs are notable for more than simply their presence in the show—the sheer magnificence of the location. The cathedral is a masterpiece of Gothic and Romanesque design, and mounting those steps feels like you're ascending to something much larger than you. Whether you're a Game of Thrones fan or not, the magnificence of it all is difficult not to be impressed with.

Exploring the King's Landing Experience

While Girona appeared in Game of Thrones as Braavos and Oldtown, one of its most notable transformations was into King's Landing—Westeros' capital and the site of all political intrigue, betrayals, and, of course, the great wildfire explosion. Exploring

Girona's streets with King's Landing in mind lends a new dimension to the city's medieval splendor.

Walking over the city's old walls, known as the Passeig de la Muralla, was a highlight of my King's Landing experience. These walls played an important role in several Game of Thrones sequences, and as I strolled along them, I couldn't help but envision myself keeping guard over the city, watching for approaching troops or possibly a dragon or two. The views from the summit are stunning, and it's clear why Girona was picked as a significant site in the series.

Exploring Girona's twisting streets, tight alleys, and magnificent squares while thinking about King's Landing gave me a fresh respect for how perfectly this city fits into the Game of Thrones universe. Whether you're strolling through Plaça dels Jurats, exploring the hidden corners of the Jewish Quarter, or crossing the Pont de Pedra, Girona's medieval atmosphere brings the world of Westeros to life in ways that few other locales can.

For Game of Thrones fans, visiting Girona is like entering another world, one filled with kings, queens, dragons, and dramatic battles. Even if you're not a die-hard fan, the Game of Thrones experience is a unique way to see this gorgeous city. And who knows? By the time you leave, you might find yourself binge-watching the entire series, hoping to get a glimpse of Girona amidst the tumult of Westeros.

Chapter 4

CULINARY DELIGHTS OF GIRONA

Let me begin by saying that if you visit Girona and do not sample its gastronomic delights, you are missing out. There's something unique about how this city, located in Catalonia's northeast corner, elevates food to an art form. Whether you're eating a rustic plate of tapas in a secluded corner or sitting down to a Michelin-starred supper, Girona makes every meal feel like a celebration. And, let's face it, nothing connects you to a location like its food.

As someone who has spent more time than I care to confess eating my way through Girona, I can confidently declare that the city knows how to dazzle with its cuisine. And it's not only the taste—though, believe me, the taste will haunt your dreams—but the complete experience: the ambiance, the passion that goes into every dish, and the sheer range of flavors that make your taste buds dance. So saddle up and join me on a culinary tour of Girona, where each meal tells a story and every mouthful is memorable.

Girona's Best Restaurants: Michelin Star Dining

When it comes to Girona's food scene, you can't deny its reputation as a Michelin-star powerhouse. In reality, this city is home to one of the world's most famous restaurants, El Celler de Can Roca, which is run by the Roca brothers and has three Michelin stars. I'm talking about a restaurant that is constantly rated among the greatest in the world. And let me tell you: the hype is real.

Getting a reservation at El Celler de Can Roca is like to attempting to get into an exclusive club, except that this club offers dishes that are virtually art on a plate. I was fortunate enough to secure a reservation after several months of searching. The encounter was mind-blowing. It wasn't just the cuisine, which was incredible—it was the entire dramatic eating experience. From the time I walked in, I was given to an immaculate exhibition of flavors, textures, and smells that challenged everything I thought I understood about food. The Roca brothers—Joan, the head chef; Josep, the sommelier; and Jordi, the pastry chef—have created an unforgettable gastronomic experience.

Don't worry if you can't obtain a reservation at El Celler; there are plenty of other fantastic restaurants in Girona. Massana, which has a Michelin star, serves a fresh interpretation on Catalan cuisine with a modern twist. I enjoyed an unforgettable lunch there, with seasonal ingredients and imaginative presentations that made me feel as if I were dining in an edible art gallery.

And for those looking for Michelin-star excellence without breaking the bank, Girona has a plethora of fine-dining options that will put you in a food coma (in the best manner imaginable). Nu is a more casual restaurant where you can try imaginative Asian-inspired dishes, whilst Divinum is recognized for its refined, seasonally driven Catalan cuisine. Girona may be modest, but its Michelin-starred restaurants punch much above their weight.

Must-try dishes include local cuisine and tapas.

If you want to get to the heart of Girona's culinary soul, you must try the local cuisine and tapas. You know, the kind of food that doesn't require eloquent words or intricate plating since the flavors speak for themselves. Girona's cuisine is steeped in Catalan traditions, with a focus on fresh ingredients, robust tastes, and a deep appreciation for the land and sea.

Let's start with escalivada, a dish that appears so simple yet packs a flavor punch that makes you wonder why you haven't been eating it your entire life. This is a meal of roasted veggies (usually eggplant, peppers, and onions), drizzled with olive oil, and served with a piece of crusty bread. It's rustic, smokey, and totally fantastic.

Then there's butifarra, a Catalan sausage that hugs your taste receptors. It's usually grilled and served with mongetes (white beans), or, if you're lucky, on a sandwich with allioli (garlic mayonnaise). This is the kind of substantial cuisine that makes you want to climb a mountain afterward—though I'd probably just go back to bed for a snooze.

And don't forget about suquet de peix, a traditional fish stew that's like a Catalan love letter to the Mediterranean. It's cooked with a combination of fish and shellfish in a rich tomato broth thickened with ground almonds. I ate this at a small family-run restaurant in Girona, and I swear I could taste the sea with every bite.

Of course, no supper in Girona is complete without tapas. This is when the real fun begins: ordering a choice of small meals to share with friends over a bottle of local wine. Patatas bravas (crispy potatoes with a spicy tomato sauce), pan con tomate (garlic and tomato bread), and calamares a la romana (fried calamari) were among my favorite tapas meals. The beauty of tapas is that it's all about sharing, which in Girona means trying a little bit of everything and never running out of reasons to order more.

Food Markets: Mercat del Lleó

If you really want to get to know a place, visit its markets. In Girona, that means going to the Mercat del Lleó, a bustling food market that has been the core of the city's culinary scene for decades. This is where locals go to buy fresh produce, meats, cheeses, and seafood, and I found myself meandering among the stalls, drooling over the sheer variety of tasty ingredients available.

The Mercat del Lleó is the type of location where you wish you had a kitchen in your hotel room since the fruit is so fresh and delicious that you'll want to cook everything yourself. Rows of bright vegetables adorn the stalls, including luscious tomatoes, blazing red peppers, and glossy eggplants that nearly beg to be cooked. And don't even get me started on the seafood—everything from plump shrimp to delicate fish, fresh from the Mediterranean and ready to cook to perfection.

One of my favorite market finds was the jamón ibérico table, where I spent a good 15 minutes watching the vendor deftly slice paper-thin pieces of cured ham. If you've never had jamón ibérico, you're missing out on one of life's greatest pleasures—a melt-in-your-mouth experience that's both luxurious and delicious.

For cheese enthusiasts (and who isn't?), the market offers a dizzying selection of native Catalan cheeses to try. I couldn't resist picking up a wedge of mató, a fresh cheese that is commonly served with honey for dessert. It's light, creamy, and the ideal sweet finish to any meal.

What's the nicest aspect about Mercat del Lleó? You can nibble your way through it. Several stalls provide ready-to-eat food, so take a mouthful of tortilla de patatas or a freshly cooked bocadillo and continue browsing the market like the genuine foodie you are.

Best Cafes and Coffee Shops in Girona

To be honest, one of my favorite aspects of travel is discovering those wonderful tiny cafés where you can sip a coffee, watch the world go by, and imagine you're a native. Girona didn't disappoint in this regard. The café culture here is vibrant, and whether you're looking for a fast cortadoor or an extravagant dessert, there's a place for you.

One of my favorite hangouts was La Fabrica, a cyclist-friendly café in the Old Town. This café, run by former professional cyclist Christian Meier and his wife Amber, is a refuge for both coffee lovers and cyclists. The environment is warm and welcoming, and the coffee—made with beans roasted in-house— is among the best I've ever had. Furthermore, the pastries are to die for. I may or may not have acquired a minor craving for their almond croissants.

For something more traditional, I recommend Cafè L'Arc, which is just in front of Girona Cathedral. Sipping a coffee with the towering cathedral in the background has a beautiful quality that makes you feel like you're living in a postcard. The coffee is wonderful, and if you're looking for something sweet, try the xuixo, a fried pastry filled with custard that is a Gironan delicacy.

For a more modern ambiance, visit Espresso Mafia, another gem operated by Christian Meier. It's minimalist, elegant, and ideal for individuals who take coffee seriously. The menu is minimal yet high-quality, and the baristas are eager to discuss their passion for coffee. Furthermore, they sell cold brew on tap, which is a godsend during Girona's sweltering summer months.

Girona's Wine & Craft Beer Scene

You may think of Spain as a land of wine, and you would be correct, but Girona also has a thriving craft beer industry that is well worth exploring. I've always been more of a wine drinker, but after spending some time in Girona, I can tell that the craft beer here is unique.

Let us start with the wine. Catalonia is famed for its DO Empordà wines, which are produced in vines immediately north of Girona. These wines, especially the reds, are strong and full of character, just like the region. During my stay, I was able to visit a couple local wineries, which was a lovely experience. The scenery—rolling hills covered in grapes, with the Pyrenees in the distance—sets the tone for some of the best wine-tasting experiences you'll ever have.

Plaça del Vi 7, a little wine bar in Girona's Old Town, is one of my favorites. Dani, the owner, is passionate about exhibiting native Catalan wines, and the list is expertly curated. Whether you prefer a clean white or a powerful red, you'll find something to suit your taste.

Now onto the artisan brew. Girona's beer scene is small but formidable, with several local breweries opening in recent years. La Calaverais is one of the most popular, recognized for its unique and experimental beers. I went to B12, a vegan craft beer pub in Girona that serves a rotating variety of local brews and a plant-based menu. It's a comfortable, unpretentious atmosphere, and the beer selection is remarkable, ranging from zesty IPAs to deep stouts.

Cooking Classes: Learn Local Recipes

If you're anything like me, you know that the best way to bring a piece of a place home is through its cuisine. Why not learn how to cook like a local while you're in Girona? During my trip, I took a cooking class, which was one of the most enjoyable (and delicious) experiences I had.

I joined up for a traditional Catalan cooking lesson, where we learnt how to prepare paella, crème catalana, and fideuà. The instructor, a Girona native, guided us through each stage of the cooking process with compassion and humor. Chopping onions and stirring a simmering pot of rice while sipping local wine is immensely enjoyable.

By the end of the lesson, we sat down to savor the fruits of our effort, and let me tell you, the paella was some of the best I've ever had. The session also included a trip to the Mercat del Lleó, where we selected fresh ingredients and learned about the significance of seasonal vegetables in Catalan cuisine.

Whether you're an expert cook or someone who can barely boil water, attending a cooking class in Girona is an excellent opportunity to immerse yourself in the local food culture and bring a taste of Catalonia home with you.

Girona's food scene is a feast for the senses, featuring everything from Michelin-starred restaurants to rustic local delicacies, all served with a side of history and culture. Whether you're drinking a cortado at a café, strolling through the Mercat del Lleó, or indulging in a wine and tapas combination, Girona's cuisine leaves an indelible impact. Just remember to pack your stretchy pants—you'll need them!

Chapter 5

ART AND CULTURE IN GIRONA

Girona is a city that wears its history and culture like a brilliantly stitched tapestry, with each thread telling a tale and each color representing the essence of this historic city. Art and culture are more than just an aspect of life in Girona; they are the life. As a traveler, it's difficult not to become swept up in the excitement of it all. Whether you're walking into a centuries-old museum or stumbling upon street art in a hidden lane, Girona has a way of making you feel like every corner is a work of beauty.

I spent a lot of time immersing myself in Girona's artistic and cultural environment, and it didn't take long for me to realize that this is a city that values creativity. It's not just about admiring what has come before (though there is plenty of that); it's about witnessing the living, breathing art and culture that are evolving alongside the city. So, take your curiosity and let's explore Girona's artistic essence.

The Museum of Art in Girona: Artistic Heritage

Let's start with the Girona Museum of Art. This museum, housed in the former Episcopal Palace, is one of those sites where you enter and immediately feel as if you're about to embark on a voyage through time. The structure itself is impressive—an architectural masterpiece that has stood tall since the 10th century. Walking through its halls, you can't help but envision the events that have occurred here throughout the years.

The museum's collection ranges from Romanesque to current works, but the Romanesque and Gothic pieces stand out the most. As someone who has always been drawn to the dramatic, I found myself admiring the sculptures and altarpieces from the medieval period. There's something about the religious iconography, with its golden halos and stoic looks, that draws you in and makes you wonder about the painters who made these masterpieces centuries ago. What was their life like? Were they aware that their work will be valued decades later?

The Apostolado de Sant Pere, a magnificent wooden sculpture from the 12th century, is one of my favorite objects in the collection. I was astounded by how the figurines appeared to emerge from the wood, with their faces etched with such precise accuracy. The museum also has an impressive collection of Baroque and Renaissance works, including some incredibly intricate religious paintings that will keep you craning your neck and staring at the details for longer than you'd care to admit.

However, the museum is not only for art historians. It is a site where everyone may admire Girona's artistic past. Whether you're a casual observer or an art enthusiast, this museum will help you better grasp the city's rich cultural roots—and may encourage you to discover more of Girona's hidden artistic gems.

Contemporary Art Spaces and Galleries

Of course, Girona isn't just about the past. The city's contemporary art culture is thriving, and for those of us who appreciate a little modern ingenuity, there are numerous galleries and art locations to visit. Casa de Cultura, for example, is one of those locations where you may go in with no expectations and leave feeling inspired. The gallery hosts alternating exhibitions of local and international artists, with an emphasis on contemporary art that pushes limits and challenges conventional wisdom.

I strolled into Casa de Cultura on a whim one afternoon and ended up in the middle of an exhibit about the relationship between light and shadow in photography. As someone who's never been very skilled with a camera, I was astounded by how something as simple as light could convert an image into something nearly otherworldly. The exhibition space is straightforward—no frills or elaborate design—but that is what makes it work. It lets the artwork speak for itself.

Visit the Bòlit Contemporary Art Center to see innovative works by Catalan artists. This is the place to go to find out what's going on in the world of avant-garde art. I remember walking through one of their exhibitions, which featured installations built completely of repurposed materials. The artist had built a collection of sculptures that appeared to have been pulled directly from a futuristic dystopia, and I couldn't help but admire the inventiveness behind them.

For those searching for something a little more private, there are other smaller galleries across the city. Espai Tònic, a tiny gallery showcasing emerging artists, is one of my personal favorites. The environment is relaxed, and the works on show are consistently thought-provoking. It's the type of location where you can talk with the artists, learn about their process, and possibly leave with a piece of art to take home (if your suitcase allows).

Girona's Festivals: Schedule Your Visit for Events

If you want to experience Girona's culture at its most lively, schedule your visit around one of the city's several festivals. Girona enjoys a good celebration, and believe me, these events are not to be missed.

One of the most notable events is Girona's annual flower festival, Temps de Flors, which takes place in May. The entire city is converted into a flowery wonderland, with beautiful flower arrangements covering every street, square, and balcony. I happened to be in Girona during the Temps de Florsone year, and it seemed like entering into a dream. Everywhere you turned, there were vivid pops of color—roses climbing the walls, flower sculptures in the parks, and even floral displays inside the Cathedral. I spent hours strolling around the city, admiring the inventiveness of the floral displays and taking more images than I'd like to admit.

The Fires de Sant Narcís, a week-long celebration in Girona honoring the city's patron saint, is a must-see event. This festival, held in late October, is a flurry of music, parades, and traditional Catalan events. One night, I found myself in the thick of a correfoc (fire run), in which participants dressed as devils danced around the streets while whirling fireworks around them. It's loud, chaotic, and slightly terrifying—but also incredibly exhilarating. If you ever get the opportunity to observe a correfoc, do not pass it up. Just make sure to wear clothing that you don't mind having singed!

Girona also holds an excellent international film festival, the Girona Film Festival, where independent filmmakers from all over the world present their work.

As a film aficionado, I spent the entire day going between screenings, exploring new films and interacting with other moviegoers. The festival offers a relaxed atmosphere, and you're likely to run encounter directors and actors during the afterparties.

Street Art in Girona: Hidden Gems

While Girona's galleries and museums provide a more traditional view of art, the city's streets feature some of the most fascinating and unexpected artistic manifestations. Girona's street art scene is dynamic and ever-changing, with murals and graffiti giving flashes of color to the city's medieval stone walls. And the best part? You don't need a map or a guide; simply meander around the city's narrow alleyways and you're sure to discover a hidden treasure or two.

Daliin's mural in Plaça de Sant Feliu is a well-known piece of street art in Girona, paying tribute to the surrealist maestro. The mural is a striking black-and-white picture of Dalí, with his distinctive mustache growing upwards in a humorous form. It's an ideal blend of Girona's cultural legacy and contemporary ingenuity.

Another highlight is the street art along the River Onyar, where local artists have turned the riverside into a vibrant canvas. I recall wandering along the river one lovely afternoon and appreciating the vibrant murals that adorned the walls. Each piece appeared to convey a unique story—some were political, some were playful, but all were indisputably artistic. One artwork in particular attracted my attention: a massive octopus wrapping its tentacles around a medieval structure. It was both odd and mesmerizing.

The best part about Girona's street art is that it is constantly changing. What you see today may not be there tomorrow, as new artists arrive and make their stamp on the city. It serves as a reminder that, like Girona, art is continuously developing.

Girona Cultural Performances: Theaters and Shows

If you want to fully immerse yourself in Girona's cultural scene, you must see a live performance at one of the city's theaters. Girona has a vibrant theatrical scene, and whether you prefer classical performances, modern plays, or something a little more experimental, there is always something happening.

The Teatre Municipal de Girona, a stunning 19th-century theater that has staged everything from opera to ballet to modern dance, is one of the city's top venues. The first time I arrived, I witnessed a Carmen performance, and the artists' passion and intensity captivated me. The theater itself is beautiful, with elegant balconies and luxurious crimson seats that transport you to another time period.

For a more personal experience, visit La Planeta, a smaller theater that specializes in contemporary and experimental acts. I once attended a one-woman play here that was both hilarious and poignant, and the small stage made me feel like I was right in the thick of it. Smaller theaters like this one have a unique vitality that radiates off the stage.

During the summer, Girona's outdoor entertainment scene comes to life, with open-air concerts and theater shows held in the city's squares and parks. El Claustre de la Catedral, the Girona Cathedral's cloister, is a particularly lovely location for performances, especially during the Nits de Clàssica festival, which brings classical music to some of the city's most stunning medieval spaces.

Music in Girona: Classical, Jazz, and Modern

Girona's music culture is as broad as its art, offering something for everyone, whether you enjoy classical, jazz, or new sounds. As a music fan, I made it a point to visit as many local music venues as possible during my stay, and I was not disappointed.

For classical music fans, Girona hosts several outstanding events, including the aforementioned Nits de Clàssica. This festival is a delight for classical music fans, with performances taking place in breathtaking sites such as the Girona Cathedral and the Monastery of Sant Pere de Galligants. I went to a concert one evening in the cathedral's cloister, and let me tell you, there's something heavenly about hearing a string quartet in a space that has stood for over a thousand years. The acoustics were superb, and the music seemed to reverberate off the ancient stone walls, sending thrills down my spine.

Sunset Jazz Club is the place to go if you want something with more groove. Tucked away in a secluded corner of the Old Town, this modest club has been holding live jazz concerts for years, and it's the ideal place to unwind with a glass of wine and some soft music. One night, I found myself sitting in the front row, watching a local group really tear it up on stage. The enthusiasm was contagious, and by the end of the night, the entire audience was tapping their feet and nodding along.

Let's not ignore Girona's modern music scene. The city hosts various indie music festivals, notably the Strenes Festival, which features emerging Catalan and Spanish acts. I went to one of the festival's open-air concerts at Plaça de Catalunya, and the atmosphere was fantastic. Standing in the heart of a throng, listening to live music against the backdrop of Girona's medieval buildings, creates a sense of belonging.

Girona's throbbing heart is art and culture, and there's no shortage of creativity here, whether you're visiting its old museums, enjoying its contemporary art, or dancing to the rhythm of its music scene. Every corner brings a new discovery, every performance a new emotion, and each mural a new perspective. Girona is a city that values artistic expression, and as a visitor, you can't help but become engrossed in its cultural charm.

Chapter 6

SHOPPING IN GIRONA

When it comes to shopping, Girona may not be the first place that comes to mind—there are no flashing neon lights or megamalls as far as the eye can see. But therein lays the appeal. Shopping in Girona is about discovering hidden jewels, finding one-of-a-kind treasures, and supporting local artisans who have been refining their trade for centuries. Whether you're looking for a hand-stitched leather bag, artisanal cheese, or a quirky antique find, this city provides a relaxed yet enjoyable shopping experience. Girona is more than just shopping; it's also about making memories.

I have to admit that I am not the type of person who spends entire days shopping while traveling (or so I tell myself), but Girona changed my mind. Strolling through its narrow alleyways, I was captivated by the boutiques, specialized shops, and market booths, all of which sold unique and locally manufactured things. Let me show you the greatest locations to buy in Girona, whether you're shopping for souvenirs, fashion, or the perfect gift to take home.

Best Shopping Streets and Areas

Let's begin with Girona's main commercial areas. Carrer de Santa Clarais should be your first stop. This lively boulevard parallels the River Onyar and is home to a variety of high-end boutiques, artisanal shops, and well-known worldwide brands. I like walking along this street in the early afternoon, when the sun creates a golden light on the buildings and the inhabitants are out for a post-lunch promenade. If you want to indulge, this is the place to do so. There's everything from trendy apparel to gorgeous jewelry, as well as some unique gift boutiques.

La Rambla de la Llibertat, just across the river, is another popular shopping destination. This lovely street is bordered with plane trees and brimming with charming cafes and shops. It's the type of street that makes you feel like you've walked into a postcard. I spent hours here, going in and out of shops and stopping at one of the several sidewalk cafes for a coffee and some people-watching. The ideal day to explore La Rambla is on Saturday, when the weekly market is in full swing. Local artisans offer everything from handcrafted jewelry to ceramics, and the mood is lively among both locals and tourists.

Barri Vell, Girona's Old Town, offers a more easygoing atmosphere. Here's where the real treasure seeking starts. The Old Town's tiny, meandering lanes are lined with one-of-a-kind boutiques and businesses that appear to have been around for a long time. Every turn reveals another hidden gem, whether it's a little shop selling hand-painted pottery or an olive oil-only establishment. Shopping in Barri Vell is about the delight of discovery rather than marking items off a list.

Souvenirs to Take Home: Locally Made Items

If you're anything like me, you can't leave a location without taking home a small bit of it. But forget about gaudy, mass-produced souvenirs—Girona has so much more authentic, locally crafted things that you'll want to bring home.

Ceramics are among the nicest items to buy in Girona. The region has a rich history of pottery, and you may find finely produced pieces in shops across the city. I purchased a couple of hand-painted bowls from Ceràmica Costa, a family-run shop in the Old Town that has been producing pottery for generations. Each piece is unique, and they make ideal mementos or gifts. Plus, every time I use those bowls at home, I get to reflect on my time in Girona.

Another traditional Catalan thing to carry home is a Caganer—and if you don't know what it is, prepare to laugh. Catalans have a unique habit of including the Caganeris figurine in their Christmas nativity scenes. The Caganer is a depiction of a person, usually a well-known individual or public figure, going about their business. Yes, that is precisely as you imagine. It's ridiculous and somehow endearing, and you can find them at shops all across Girona. I purchased a couple Caganers as gag gifts for friends, and they were a huge hit.

Don't leave Girona without trying Taps de Cadaqués, a traditional sweet delight shaped like a cork and composed of almond dough. They're excellent, and after you try them, you'll wonder why you didn't buy more.

Girona's Boutiques: Clothing and Accessories

Girona's fashion is effortlessly stylish, as one would expect from a Catalan city. The shops here provide a welcome departure from the cookie-cutter retailers found in larger towns. Girona's fashion culture is dedicated about promoting local designers and independent companies, so expect to find something genuinely unique.

Noir et Blanc, a minimalist apparel boutique that focuses in timeless designs with a modern touch, was one of my favorites. I spent much too long trying on flowy linen skirts and lovely tops, finally leaving with a stunning scarf that I now wear far more frequently than I should. The atmosphere here is very much "effortless cool," and the quality is excellent.

For accessories, Cocco BCN is the way to go. This business specialized in handmade leather products, and I couldn't resist purchasing a wonderfully created handbag. The craftsmanship was exceptional, and I appreciated knowing that I was supporting a local artisan. Plus, let's be honest—there's something about a leather purse that makes you feel like you've got it all together, even if you don't.

If you want something a little more daring, go to Caboclo, a store that blends fashion and ecology. Their shoes and accessories are crafted from recycled materials, and each has a distinct, earthy look. I departed with a pair of sandals that are now my go-to for every summer vacation.

Specialty Shops: Cheese, Olive Oil, and More

Girona is an expert in food. And browsing for unique foods in Girona is almost as enjoyable as eating them. There are numerous businesses dedicated to local delicacies, ranging from artisanal cheeses to olive oil, and believe me, you'll want to bring some of these pleasures home with you.

Let's begin with cheese—because who doesn't adore cheese? Girona produces some of the greatest Catalan cheeses, and there are numerous specialty shops where you may try and purchase them. La Formatgeria de Girona is one such location. The shop is small but packed with a well picked assortment of cheeses, many of which are produced locally in the surrounding area. The proprietor is passionate about cheese and will gladly provide samples till you select your favorite. I left with a wheel of Garrotxa, a semi-cured goat cheese with a subtle, nutty flavour. It was difficult not to eat the whole thing on the train journey home.

Then there's olive oil. Catalonia produces some of the world's best olive oil, and Girona is the ideal place to stock up. Oleoteca Girona is a specialized boutique dedicated just to olive oil, and it is a must-stop for every foodie. The staff is quite knowledgable and will walk you through a sampling of their many oils, ranging from powerful and peppery to smooth and delicious. I ended up purchasing a bottle of organic extra virgin olive oil, which I now use on everything from salads to roasted vegetables.

If you have a sweet craving, visit Xocolateria Antiga, which specializes in artisanal chocolates and traditional desserts. I purchased a box of panellets, which are miniature almond cakes popular in Catalonia, as well as a bar of chocolate infused with local spices. We'll just say they didn't last long.

Antique Stores and Flea Markets

One of my favorite things about Girona is its sense of history—and you can bring a piece of it home with you by visiting the city's many antique shops and flea markets. Whether you're looking for an antique trinket, a one-of-a-kind piece of furniture, or a dusty old book, Girona has lots of places to find something with a story.

Antiguitats Alfons is one of the city's most well-known antique shops, and entering it is like entering a time capsule. The shop is packed with everything from ancient furniture to old photographs, and you could easily spend hours browsing the mounds of oddities. I walked out with a little, hand-carved wooden box that appeared to have been snatched directly from a fairytale. It currently rests on my bedside table, containing my most treasured possessions.

If you're in Girona on the first Saturday of the month, don't miss the Rambla Flea Market, where people put up stalls offering antiques, vintage things, and other unique finds. The market has a relaxed atmosphere, and there's something immensely satisfying about negotiating for a good deal on an ancient Spanish tapestry or a bundle of antique postcards. I purchased a vintage mantón de Manila (a traditional embroidered silk shawl) for a fraction of the price I would have paid in a boutique.

Shopping Malls and Department Stores

If you are a conventional shopper who prefers the convenience of having everything under one roof, Girona has a few shopping malls and department stores to meet your needs. Espai Gironès is the city's largest mall, located just outside Salt's city center. All of the typical suspects can be found here, including fashion labels, gadgets, home items, and a good range of eateries. It's not the best spot to find local treasures, but it's ideal if you're looking for something specific or want to peruse a variety of places at once.

El Corte Inglés in Girona provides a more upmarket shopping experience, with a broad selection of luxury brands, cosmetics, and fashion. It's essentially Spain's version of Bloomingdale's, and if you're looking for some high-end shopping therapy, this is the place to go. I ended up roaming through the cosmetics aisle and leaving with a bag full of goods I absolutely needed (or so I convinced myself at the time).

Girona may not be the world's shopping capital, but that's what makes it so unique. The city's stores, boutiques, and marketplaces provide a personalized, genuine, and characterful experience. Shopping in Girona is all about the excitement of discovery, whether you're looking for a one-of-a-kind memento, sampling local specialties, or exploring for antique finds. And who knows. You might just leave with something you didn't realize you needed—but can't live without.

Chapter 7

DAY TRIPS FROM GIRONA

Let me tell you, as much as I love Girona (and could easily spend weeks strolling its medieval alleyways), it was the day tours from the city that elevated my experience. Girona is the ideal starting point for discovering Catalonia's most beautiful landscapes, historic attractions, and quirky jewels. There's a day excursion for everyone, whether you want to enjoy the Mediterranean heat, climb through old volcanic terrain, or immerse yourself in Salvador Dalí's bizarre universe.

I'm not one to stay around for long, so I made it a point to get out of Girona as often as possible, and let me tell you, I was not disappointed. Each day trip felt like a new chapter in my Catalan vacation, with an entirely different vibe than the city. So, grab your sunscreen, hiking boots, or whatever else you might need, and let's go over some of the best day trips from Girona.

Costa Brava: Exploring the Mediterranean Coast

First up is the Costa Brava, one of the most magnificent coastline places I've ever seen. If you fantasize about brilliant blue waves, steep cliffs, and tiny fishing villages, Costa Brava is your utopia. It's only a 30-minute drive from Girona, making it an ideal spot for a sunny day excursion.

My journey began in Tossa de Mar, a picturesque coastal town with an old medieval fortress that appears to have been taken directly from a fairytale. Consider this: golden dunes, lapping seas, and a castle situated on a hill above it all. That is Tossa de Mar. I spent the morning walking along the historic city walls, pausing every few meters to enjoy the panoramic views of the Mediterranean. And, yeah, I imagined myself as a medieval warrior guarding the fortress—though, with sunscreen in hand, it wasn't as spectacular as I'd planned.

However, the true charm of Costa Brava comes in its craggy shoreline. After Tossa de Mar, I drove a short distance north to Cala del Pi, one of the most beautiful tiny bays I have ever seen. The water in this photo is so clear that it appears to have been enhanced in Photoshop. I swam, sunbathed, and even tried snorkeling. There's something quite liberating about floating in the Mediterranean, with the sun on your face and nothing but the sound of waves breaking against the cliffs.

If you want to explore rather than relax, there are numerous coastal walking pathways that will take you to secret coves and isolated beaches. I trekked a portion of the Cami de Ronda, a trail that snakes along the coast, providing breathtaking views around every bend. Costa Brava is one of those spots where you feel like you've discovered heaven.

Banyoles Lake: A Relaxing Getaway

After a few days of visiting Girona and the coast, I needed something more relaxing. Enter Banyoles Lake, a lovely freshwater lake located about 20 minutes from Girona by automobile. This location is the epitome of a tranquil getaway. When I arrived, I felt as if I had left the world behind and entered a Zen-like oasis of serenity.

The lake is vast, and it is surrounded by thick flora, making it ideal for a leisurely stroll or a bike ride. I decided to rent a bike and spend the morning riding around the lake, stopping at lovely spots along the route to take photos or simply rest and observe the soothing ripples of the water. One of my favorite aspects of Banyoles is that it appears to be unaffected by the craziness of modern life—there were no crowds or cars, just the sound of birds and the occasional paddleboarder skimming across the lake.

Paddleboarding is another great way to explore Banyoles. I rented a paddleboard for an hour and had a fantastic time drifting over the water, taking in the views of the surrounding hills. If you're not into water activities, don't worry—the lake has plenty of small nooks where you can spread out a picnic blanket and relax.

I had lunch at Can Xabanet, a quiet restaurant beside the lake, where I ate arròs negre (black rice with squid ink). It was the ideal conclusion to a morning spent in nature. Banyoles Lake is the perfect place to unwind after a day of sightseeing and reconnect with nature in its purest form.

Figueres and Dalí Museum

The Dalí Theatre-Museum in Figueres is a must-see for anybody visiting Catalonia, regardless of their interest in surrealism. The Salvador Dalí Museum in Figueres pays tribute to the artist's talent. A 40-minute journey from Girona, this day trip immersed us in Dalí's surreal world.

The museum itself is as strange as you might anticipate. From the moment you see the big eggs on the roof, you know you're in for something amazing. Inside, the experience is pure Dalí—surreal, quirky, and occasionally unnerving. I strolled through rooms adorned with his paintings, sculptures, and installations, many of which defy logic and interpretation. The museum has a section dedicated to Dalí's optical illusions. I spent too much time trying to determine if I was gazing at a woman's face or a collection of random things organized in a way that tricks the eye.

One of the highlights for me was the Mae West Room, which features furniture designed to resemble Mae West's face when viewed from a certain angle. It's unusual, whimsical, and very Dalí.

After viewing the museum and contemplating Dalí's bizarre world, I ventured into Figueres. It's a quaint small town with plenty of cafes where you can sit and ponder on the chaos you've just experienced. I had a cortado at Café Dalicatessen, a unique spot that embraces all things Dalí, before traveling back to Girona, still buzzing from the event.

La Garrotxa: Hiking in the Volcanic Region

If you enjoy nature as I do, La Garrotxa Volcanic Zone Natural Park is a must-see destination. This region, located about an hour from Girona, is known for its extinct volcanoes and lush woods, and it is one of Catalonia's top hiking destinations.

My expedition began in the town of Olot, which serves as the entryway to La Garrotxa. From there, I set out on a climb to Volcà del Croscat, one of the park's most famous volcanoes. Before you get visions of pouring lava and violent eruptions, let me assure you that these volcanoes have not been active for thousands of years. Instead, you'll be strolling through serene woodlands and across volcanic craters that have been overgrown by vegetation.

The trail to Volcà del Croscat was surprisingly easy, even for someone like me who frequently trips over their own feet. The environment is reminiscent of a fantasy story, with undulating hills, forests of beech trees, and the occasional blackened rock reminding you of the region's volcanic beginnings. Along the route, I came across charming stone farmhouses, some of which have been converted into guesthouses for visitors who want to spend longer time in the park.

One of the most unique experiences in La Garrotxa is a visit to the Santa Margarida Volcano, which features a modest Romanesque chapel constructed right in the crater. Yes, you read that correctly: a chapel inside a volcano. It's a short trek to the summit, and standing in the center of the crater, surrounded by the volcano's verdant slopes, is one of those times when you feel linked to something far larger than yourself.

La Garrotxa is also noted for its Fageda d'en Jordà, a magnificent beech forest that seems like something out of a fairytale. Walking into the forest seemed like entering another universe, where the sun shines through the trees in golden beams and everything is quiet and serene. If you want a day excursion that combines adventure, history, and nature, La Garrotxa is the ideal destination.

Pals and Peratallada: Medieval Villages

If you love gorgeous medieval villages (and who doesn't?), you must visit Palsand Peratallada. These two villages, approximately 40 minutes from Girona, feel like stepping back in time, with cobblestone lanes, ivy-covered stone buildings, and lovely squares. I half expected a knight in sparkling armor to come around each corner.

I began the day in Pals, a hilly community with breathtaking views of the surrounding landscape. When I walked through the ancient stone gate, I felt as if I had been transported to another age. The streets are tiny and twisting, with medieval buildings and quaint little stores selling ceramics and handcrafted goods. I spent about an hour getting lost in the maze of lanes, discovering hidden courtyards and ascending to the top of the historic Torre de les Hores, a watchtower with panoramic views of the countryside.

Next, I visited Peratallada, which may be one of the best-preserved medieval villages I've ever seen. This village is smaller and calmer than Pals, yet it is equally enchanting. The name Peratalladameans means "carved stone," and as you walk around the village, you'll understand why—many of the buildings and streets are literally cut out of the rock. It's one of those places where you feel like you've stumbled upon a timeless treasure.

Lunch at Peratallada was the highlight of the day. I discovered a small restaurant called Can Bonay, where I sat in a sun-dappled courtyard and ate pa amb tomàquet (bread with tomato) and butifarra (Catalan sausage) while sipping a glass of local red wine. It was the ideal conclusion to a day spent traveling through the past.

Montserrat Monastery: A Spiritual Escape

For a more spiritual experience, visit the Montserrat Monastery, which is about an hour and a half from Girona. Perched high in the mountains, this Benedictine abbey is one of Catalonia's most well-known religious landmarks, and it's simple to see why. When you see the jagged summits of Montserrat (which means "serrated mountain" in Catalan), you'll understand why it's been a pilgrimage destination for centuries.

The travel to Montserrat is half the fun—whether you drive or take the cable car up the mountain, the scenery is breathtaking. When you reach the summit, you'll be met by a magnificent monastery perched among the steep rocks. The basilica houses the famed Black Madonna, a wooden statue of the Virgin Mary said to have extraordinary powers. Even if you are not religious, there is something undeniably compelling about being in front of this old statue, surrounded by pilgrims and tourists from all over the world.

But Montserrat is more than just a monastery. The neighboring mountains are crisscrossed by hiking routes, providing some of Catalonia's most breathtaking views. I walked up to Sant Jeroni, Montserrat's highest peak, and the 360-degree views from there were amazing. On a clear day, you can see all the way to Barcelona, and Montserrat's jagged peaks appear to be from a dream.

Girona is an excellent base for visiting some of Catalonia's most beautiful and unusual places, with each day excursion providing an entirely new experience. Day vacations are ideal for exploring the Costa Brava, hiking through volcanic landscapes, or immersing yourself in Salvador Dalí's strange universe. Just be prepared—you might want to extend your stay (or, in my case, never leave at all).

Chapter 8

OUTDOOR ADVENTURES IN GIRONA

When it comes to outdoor activities, Girona is like a kid in a candy store—you don't know where to begin. This city, with its breathtaking landscapes, rivers, mountains, and expansive skies, virtually begs you to put on your hiking boots, grab a paddle, or hop on a bike and explore. And, believe me, after a few days of eating tapas and drinking wine in Girona's cafés, your body will be grateful for some fresh air and exercise.

I've always been the type of tourist who enjoys combining food and culture with some adventure, and Girona proved to be the ideal playground. Whether you're an adrenaline fanatic or simply seeking for a tranquil stroll through nature, Girona has outdoor activities to meet your needs—and leave you with stories to tell. Allow me to guide you through some of the best outdoor excursions available in and around this bustling city.

Hiking trails in Girona

Girona is an incredible paradise for hikers. The city is surrounded by hills, forests, and rivers, providing a variety of hiking trails suitable for everyone from casual walkers to extreme trekkers. The Sant Miquel walk is one of Girona's most popular hikes, leading to the Castell de Sant Miquel, a historic ruined fortress built on a hilltop just outside the city.

The hike is modest and takes you through woods of oak and pine trees, with the sound of birds and the occasional breeze whispering through the leaves. It's one of those routes that makes you feel like you're miles away from society, yet being only a short distance from Girona's city center. After roughly an hour of trekking, you reach the summit, where the views are simply stunning. From the top, you can see the entire city of Girona spread out below, with the snow-capped Pyrenees in the background. I recall sitting there for a while, taking everything in, and thinking, "This is exactly what I needed."

If you want something more challenging, head to the Gavarres Mountains, which are just south of Girona. The routes here are more challenging, taking you through deep forests, crossing streams, and occasionally clambering over rocks. My favorite climb in the Gavarres was to Els Àngels, a hilltop refuge with panoramic views of the surrounding landscape. The trek is a little difficult in sections, but the views from the summit make it all worthwhile. Additionally, there is a tiny café at the sanctuary where you may treat yourself with a coffee or a refreshing drink before returning down.

Kayaking in the River Ter

If you're searching for a water-based experience, kayaking down the River Teris is a must. The river flows just north of Girona and provides a tranquil and scenic route for exploring the area's natural beauties. I've kayaked many locations, but there's something special about kayaking down the Ter, with the lush green banks on each side and the occasional heron or kingfisher flying low over the water.

I scheduled a guided kayaking trip with a local tour operator, and it turned out to be one of the highlights of my stay in Girona. We started at Colomers, a little village about 20 minutes from Girona, and paddled down the river at our slow pace. The guide was excellent, pointing out wildlife, describing the history of the area, and even providing us insider information on the greatest hidden gems to explore in Girona.

The water was peaceful, with the only sound being the smooth splash of paddles diving into the river. At one point, we pulled our kayaks onto the bank and had a picnic under a tree, replete with local cheese, bread, and homemade fuet (Catalan sausage). It was one of those simple but wonderful moments that I'll always remember.

More experienced kayakers will find sections of the River Ter more challenging, with quicker currents and several small rapids. But, for me, the moderate pace was ideal, giving me enough of time to admire the view and soak in the peacefulness of the river.

Cycling Routes: Girona's Cycling Legacy

Girona is widely regarded as a cyclist's paradise. In fact, the city is recognized as Spain's "cycling capital" and is a popular training area for professional riders. But don't be intimidated—whether you're an expert or a casual rider like me, Girona has cycling courses for all skill levels.

The ride to Els Àngels, a mountaintop refuge also accessible by hiking, is a popular route. The route goes up through the countryside, providing stunning vistas of the vineyards and olive fields below. I'll be honest—this path is a bit of a climb, and there were times when I questioned my life choices as I huffed and puffed my way up the hill. But once you reach the top and witness the breathtaking vistas, it's all worthwhile. Furthermore, the descent back down is pure joy, with smooth roads and plenty of hairpin curves that make you feel like you're flying.

If you want something a little easier, consider the Vies Verdes, a network of disused railway lines that have been converted into bike lanes. These routes are largely flat and pass through some of Catalonia's most stunning scenery. I cycled from Girona to Sant Feliu de Guíxols, a coastal village approximately 40 kilometers distant. It was one of the most relaxed and picturesque rides I've done. The trail leads through forests, across rivers, and even through a few tiny settlements where you may stop for a coffee or a snack.

And, if you're feeling very daring, you may try some of the more difficult mountain routes that the experts train on. There's nothing quite like pedaling up the Rocacorbaclimb and knowing you're sharing the roads with some of the world's top riders. Just be prepared for some substantial elevation—and perhaps bring an extra energy bar or two.

Hot Air Balloon Rides Over The City

If you want to see Girona from an entirely different perspective, take a hot air balloon flight. I've always been dubious about hot air balloons, as the idea of floating hundreds of feet in the air with only a basket and a large balloon sounded a bit dangerous. But after hearing so many positive reviews, I decided to try it.

I'm so glad I did.

The experience of softly drifting above Girona and the surrounding countryside was very amazing. We took off shortly after sunrise, and seeing the city below shrink as we soared into the sky was surreal. The view from above is unlike anything I've ever seen—rolling hills, sunflower fields, the Pyrenees in the distance, and Girona's old town spread out like a little model hamlet. The light was warm and golden, and everything seemed calm and tranquil.

Our pilot was excellent, pointing us landmarks and explaining how the wind would determine where we floated. At one point, we drifted over the River Ter, watching kayakers paddle beneath us. I couldn't help but feel a little superior, thinking, "Yeah, kayaking is enjoyable, but this? "This is something entirely different."

After approximately an hour of drifting through the sky, we landed in a field where a breakfast spread greeted us, replete with cava (Catalan sparkling wine), since what's a hot air balloon journey without some bubbly to celebrate?

Rock Climbing and Adventure Sports

If you're the type of visitor who thrives on adrenaline, Girona has a lot to offer in terms of rock climbing and adventure activities. The harsh topography surrounding the city is ideal for climbing, with craggy cliffs and rocky outcrops that give ample obstacles for climbers of all skill levels.

The Cingles de Sant Roc, a magnificent limestone cliff just outside the town of Amer, is one of the top climbing destinations around Girona. The climbing routes here are diverse, ranging from beginner-friendly to more advanced climbs that demand technical skill. I'm no expert climber, but I went on a guided climbing session with a local guide, and it turned out to be one of the most thrilling experiences of my trip. It's tremendously satisfying to reach the summit of a climb, look out over the valley below, and realize you've conquered a rock face.

If rock climbing isn't your style, Girona offers a variety of other adventure activities. Canyoning in the adjacent Guilleries Massif involves rappelling down waterfalls and scrambling through narrow valleys. If you prefer something more fast-paced, you may go white-water rafting on the Noguera Pallaresa River, which is one of the top rafting places in Catalonia.

Birdwatching at Girona's Wetlands

For those who prefer a more relaxed outdoor experience, Girona's Aiguamolls de l'Empordàwetlands are a birdwatching paradise. Located just a short drive from the city, this natural park is home to a broad assortment of bird species, making it a must-see for wildlife lovers.

I've never considered myself a birdwatcher, but there's something really peaceful about spending a morning in the marshes with binoculars in hand, watching herons, storks, and even the rare flamingo go about their business. The park features a number of paths and observation sites where you can see various species depending on the time of year.

I went in the spring, which is one of the greatest seasons for birdwatching in the region. The wetlands were bustling with activity, and I saw everything from white storks nesting in the tall grass to graceful egrets wading in the shallow waters. Something about watching birds in their natural habitat causes you to slow down and appreciate the beauty of nature in a manner that is difficult to articulate.

If you're lucky, you might even see one of the park's more elusive inhabitants, such as the purple heron or Montagu's harrier. Even if you are not a bird aficionado, the tranquil ambiance of the wetlands provides an ideal respite from the rush and bustle of Girona.

Horseback Riding Tours: Scenic Rides

Finally, if you want a more relaxing outdoor excursion, consider taking a horseback riding tour in Girona's countryside. There's something extremely tranquil about riding through fields and forests on horseback, with the only sounds being the clopping of hooves on the ground and the occasional snort from your loyal mount.

I joined a small group tour that brought us through the Empordà region, located just north of Girona. Our guide was a local horse trainer who knew the area like the back of his hand, and he took us through some of the most breathtaking scenery I've ever witnessed. We rode through vineyards, olive orchards, and meandering country roads strewn with wildflowers. We even stopped at a little hilltop village to tie up the horses and eat a picnic lunch with views all the way to the coast.

Whether you are an expert rider or a total beginner, horseback riding in Girona is an unforgettable experience. The horses are kind and well-trained, and the guides do an excellent job of ensuring everyone's comfort. Plus, there's something inherently romantic about riding across the countryside on horseback—it feels like you've stepped back in time.

Outdoor excursions in Girona provide an ideal balance of excitement, relaxation, and connection to nature. There are numerous opportunities to experience the beauty and thrill of the great outdoors, like climbing up to old castles, kayaking down a quiet river, and soaring above the city in a hot air balloon. Girona is well-known for its history and culture, but its natural settings are equally captivating—and the adventures you'll have here will leave you with lifelong memories (and maybe a few aching muscles).

Chapter 9

GIRONA'S PARKS AND GARDENS

Girona, a city noted for its ancient splendor and centuries-old stone walls, pleasantly surprises visitors with its wealth of lush green spaces and attractive gardens. I can't tell you how many times I've stepped off a busy street into a park and felt as if I'd entered another world—one filled with birdsong and the delicate rustle of leaves. Girona's parks and gardens have something for everyone, whether you want to relax, go for a run, or just take in some fresh air.

Let's take a tour around some of Girona's most lovely outdoor settings, where history meets nature and peace is only a bench away.

Parc de la Devesa, Girona's Green Heart

If Girona had lungs, they would certainly be at Parc de la Devesa. The city's largest park invites relaxation and contemplation. Walking around the park's vast, tree-lined pathways, you can't help but feel relaxed. I'm not sure if it's the towering plane trees—some of which are over 150 years old—or the quiet crunch of leaves underfoot, but there's something about La Devesa that calms the soul.

The park covers approximately 40 hectares, but it does not feel overwhelming. It's like a green oasis in the heart of Girona, ideal for getting away from the city's congestion. On any given day, you'll see families enjoying picnics, joggers making their way around the trails, and couples strolling hand in hand. I found myself spending a lot of time here, especially in the late afternoon when the golden sunshine streams through the leaves, creating an ethereal glow that makes everything appear like a scene from a movie.

One of the features of Parc de la Devesa is the weekly market. Every Tuesday and Saturday, the park comes alive with vendors selling fresh food, clothing, and other locally sourced things. It's a sensory explosion in the nicest way possible—the aromas of fresh herbs and baked products, the sound of sellers screaming out their wares, and the sight of people scurrying around looking for their next big purchase. I may have gone beyond and purchased more cheese and olives than I could possibly devour, but let's just say I don't regret it.

Jardins dels Alemanys: A Garden of History

For a completely different vibe, visit the Jardins dels Alemanys, a garden that combines history and nature. The Jardins dels Alemanys, located in Girona's Old Town, are part of the ancient Girona Wall, which was built in Roman times. Walking through this garden feels like you've discovered a secret realm buried beyond the city's stone defenses.

I first noticed Jardins dels Alemanys while wandering along the city walls, and I was immediately taken by its peaceful beauty. Unlike Girona's more manicured parks, this garden has a little untamed, unkempt feel—as if nature had gradually reclaimed the place over the years. Olive trees, cypresses, and creeping ivy appear to spill over the walls, creating a poetic effect. What about the viewpoints? Incredible. From various spots in the garden, you can view across the Old Town's rooftops and out to the distant mountains.

The garden's name, Alemanys, refers to the German soldiers stationed in Girona during the siege in 1653. While the garden is a calm escape, walking along its trails makes you feel connected to the city's past. It's the type of location where you can sit on a stone bench with a book (or, in my case, a ham and cheese sandwich) and lose track of time.

What I liked best about Jardins dels Alemanys was how quiet it was, even on busy days. It's like a tiny refuge in the heart of the city, where you can withdraw and collect your thoughts—or, if you're like me, simply sit and think about what life may have been like in medieval Girona.

Parc del Migdia: Relax and Unwind

If Parc de la Devesa is Girona's magnificent, majestic park, Parc del Migdia is its cool, laid-back counterpart. This park, located just outside of the city center, has a more modern vibe, with huge lawns, a central pond, and lots of shady spaces to spread out a blanket and rest. Parc del Migdiaon became one of my favorite places to relax after I discovered it on a particularly sunny afternoon.

What I like about this park is how it's intended to accommodate everyone. There is a large playground for children, a skate park for teenagers, and plenty of seats and grassy places for those of us who like to sit quietly and people-watch. The park is extremely popular with residents, and you'll frequently find groups of friends sitting on the grass, chatting and basking in the sun. I joined them, finding a seat under a tree to read my latest novel while sipping an ice-cold horchata (a traditional Spanish drink prepared with tiger nuts).

A calm pond in the park's center is flanked by weeping willows and strolling paths. It's the kind of location where you can take a vacation from the outside world and watch ducks paddle slowly across the water. I found myself returning to Parc del Migdia anytime I wanted a break from sightseeing—a peaceful oasis where I could recharge before returning to the city.

Montjuïc Castle & Gardens

The Montjuïc Castle and Gardens are a must-see for those seeking a historical backdrop to their garden. Montjuïc Castle, perched on a hill overlooking Girona, offers both amazing views of the city and a quiet garden that feels worlds away from the urban bustle.

The trek to Montjuïc is physically demanding, but the reward is well worth it. As you climb the hill, you'll pass through a series of tiered gardens filled with Mediterranean flora like lavender, rosemary, and olive trees, all of which seem to thrive in Catalonia's warm climate. The gardens are immaculately kept, and the aroma of herbs permeates the air as you walk through the paths.

Montjuïc Castle, a 17th-century fortification, is located at the top. The castle is impressive, and you can tour its towers, walls, and dungeons, but the real highlight is the vista. From the top of the castle, you can see all of Girona, including the Pyrenees in the distance. It's one of those moments when you just have to pause and soak it all in—partly because you're out of breath from the climb, and partly because the scenery is absolutely breathtaking.

After exploring the castle, I spent some time in the gardens, enjoying the peace and quiet while viewing the city below. There's something about being up there, surrounded by history and nature, that makes you feel like you've discovered a hidden gem of Girona that few people are aware of.

River Walks Along The Onyar

One of my favorite aspects of Girona was its riverbank charm, and there's no better way to experience it than to take a leisurely walk along the River Onyar. The river flows through the heart of the city, and its banks are dotted with colorful buildings, old bridges, and lots of places to sit and watch the world go by.

I found myself walking by the river practically every day, especially in the early morning when the light was gentle and golden. There's something amazing about seeing Girona's iconic casas de colores—the vividly painted houses that border the river—reflect on the water's surface. It's one of those famous sites that appears even more stunning in person.

The Pont de Pedra, one of the several bridges across the Onyar, provides some of the best views of the city's old and new sides mixing together. I'd frequently pause here to admire the view or take a few shots (because, let's be honest, the view is too wonderful not to share on Instagram).

For a longer walk, take the riverfront trails that lead out of the city center and into the surrounding countryside. One of my favorite hikes was along the Camí Ral, which follows the river through fields and woodlands, providing a pleasant getaway from the city. It is an excellent way to get some fresh air and exercise while seeing Girona's natural beauty.

Botanical Gardens Around Girona

Girona also has various botanical gardens that display the region's unique plant life. They're ideal for anyone who appreciates the beauty of nature—or, in my case, likes to pretend they know the difference between a fern and a ficus.

The Marimurtra Botanical Garden, set on the cliffs overlooking the Costa Brava, is just outside the city limits. This garden is a bit of a journey from Girona, but it's definitely worth it. Marimurtrais is one of the most important botanical gardens in the Mediterranean, with more than 4,000 plant species from all over the world. As I went around the garden's twisting walkways, I was struck by the vast diversity of plants, from towering palms to delicate orchids. What about the viewpoints? Absolutely stunning. The garden's location on the cliffs provides breathtaking views of the Mediterranean, with the sound of waves breaking below as you explore.

Closer to Girona, you'll find the Jardins de Cap Roig, another breathtaking floral garden that combines art, nature, and history. The gardens are positioned on a hill overlooking the sea and are well-known for their collection of Mediterranean flora, sculptures, and art pieces. I spent the entire afternoon roaming through the gardens, appreciating the flowers and relaxing in the tranquil ambiance. There's something really peaceful about being surrounded by so much greenery, with the sea wind gently rustling through the leaves.

Girona's parks and gardens provide an ideal escape from the city's hectic streets, allowing you to unwind, explore, and reconnect with nature. Girona has a green area for anyone, whether you want to read a book in peace, take a beautiful walk along the river, or visit a garden rich in history and beauty. It's the kind of spot where you can take a deep breath, feel the sun on your face, and enjoy the basic pleasures of being in nature.

Chapter 10

GIRONA BY NIGHT

Girona by day is breathtaking, with its medieval buildings, lovely squares, and lively ambiance. But at night? The city morphs into something nearly magical. It's as if Girona has two personalities: one that thrives during the day, with its bustling markets and sun-soaked streets, and one that comes alive after dark, when the cobblestone streets are bathed in the warm glow of street lamps and the city's pubs and nightclubs call with promises of fun. And believe me when I say that Girona has a lot to offer after the sun goes down.

During my time in Girona, I realized that the nightlife involves more than just going to clubs and partying till dawn. The city provides a variety of activities, from calm, romantic walks around the Old Town to late-night tapas and live music that will keep you tapping your feet till the early hours. Girona has something for everyone, whether you prefer a night out or a more relaxed evening. Let me show you what makes this city so enchanting after dark.

Best Bars and Nightclubs in Girona

Let's start with the pubs, as Girona has enough of them. Whether you're looking for craft cocktails, a glass of local wine, or an ice-cold beer, there's something for you. Nykteri's Cocktail Bar, a quaint little location tucked away in the Old Town, was one of my favorites for starting the night. This location feels like it came straight out of a movie—it's dark and intimate, with leather armchairs and a bar filled with every liquor imaginable. The bartenders here are amazing artists, crafting some of the most inventive cocktails I've ever had. I requested something "fruity but not too sweet," and the drink I received was ideal—bright, refreshing, and with just the right amount of bite.

If you enjoy beer, B12 is the place to be. This vegan pub is well-known for its diverse variety of craft beers, both local and worldwide. The atmosphere is easygoing and inviting, making it an ideal place to catch up with friends or make new ones. I spent a large portion of one evening conversing with the bartender about the various beers on tap, and by the time I left, I felt like I'd learned more about hops and brewing than I ever imagined possible.

For a more lively atmosphere, visit Lapsus Café. During the day, it is a relaxed café, but at night, it transforms into one of the city's most popular bars. The music here is always on point, with a mix of indie, rock, and electronic tunes that create a lively atmosphere. And if you want to dance, Lapsusha has you covered—there's always a little space to bust out some moves.

If dancing is your top priority, then Sala Yeah! Indie Club is Girona's go-to nightlife. This establishment is famous among residents for its varied mix of indie, rock, and alternative music. It's the type of place where you can let loose and dance the night away with no worries in the world. I wound up here one Saturday night, and let's just say things got a little crazy. There's something about singing along to your favorite songs with people who share your enthusiasm that makes for a great night.

Evening Strolls and Romantic Spots

However, every night in Girona does not have to be spent in the bars. Sometimes you just want to take it leisurely and appreciate the beauty of the city under the skies. And let me tell you, Girona at night is quite lovely. There's something about the small, cobblestone streets, the soft glow of the street lamps, and the deep hush that settles over the city when the day's people depart. It's as if the entire city is talking to you, begging you to discover its hidden nooks.

One of my favorite nighttime activities was going for a walk along the River Onyar. The colorful structures that surround the river are even more stunning at night, as their reflections sparkle in the water. I would frequently begin my walk at the Pont de Pedra, a stone bridge that provides one of the greatest views of the city's illuminated cityscape. From there, I'd go along the riverbank, passing the famed red iron bridge created by Gustave Eiffel. The contrast between the industrial feel of the bridge and the medieval elegance of the Old Town is most noticeable after dark.

If you're looking for something genuinely unique, head up to the Passeig de la Muralla, the ancient city walls that provide panoramic views of Girona. Walking along the walls at night, with the city stretched out before you and the stars twinkling overhead, is like entering a dream. It's ideal for a romantic evening, whether you're with a lover or simply enjoying some quiet time alone.

Plaça de la Independència is another excellent place to go for an evening stroll if you want to learn about history. This enormous square, with its fine arcades and central monument, is brilliantly illuminated at night, and there's something undeniably romantic about sitting in one of the outdoor cafés, enjoying a glass of wine, and watching the world go by.

Night Tours of Girona's Landmarks

If you are a history enthusiast like myself, you will enjoy Girona's night tours. Seeing the city's landmarks during the day is one thing; witnessing them at night, when they are illuminated and covered in shadows, is quite another. It's as if the city's history comes to life after dark, making the stories of Girona's past feel even more vivid.

One of my favorite experiences was a nighttime visit of Girona Cathedral. The cathedral is stunning enough during the day, but at night, it is quite breathtaking. The large stone steps leading up to the entryway are lit from below, creating dramatic shadows that make you feel as if you're about to enter an epic medieval story. Our guide escorted us into the cathedral, explaining its history, architecture, and the several sieges it has endured throughout the ages. Standing in a centuries-old church in the dark, guided only by the subtle flicker of candles, is very atmospheric.

Another excellent night tour option is the Jewish Quarter Ghost Tour. This trip takes you through Girona's medieval Jewish Quarter, the Call Jueu, and introduces you to some of the city's most haunting legends. As we walked through Girona's tight, winding alleyways, our guide told us stories about spooky apparitions, inexplicable disappearances, and the Jewish community's hidden history. I'll admit, there were a few times when the hairs on the back of my neck sprang up—but only in the greatest way.

Live Music Venues for a Fun Night

One of my favorite aspects about Girona is its strong support for live music. Whether you prefer jazz, rock, or something a little more experimental, there is always a place where you can see a fantastic live performance. Sunset Jazz Club is a tiny, softly lighted club that feels like something out of a 1940s noir film. The music here is exceptional, featuring performances by both local and international jazz musicians. I spent a few evenings here, sipping Rioja and listening to the soothing sounds of the saxophone. It's the type of location where time appears to slow down and you can completely lose yourself in the music.

For a more upbeat atmosphere, visit La Mirona, one of Girona's largest live music venues. This venue hosts everything from rock and indie bands to electronic DJ sets, and it is always throbbing with energy. I saw a local indie band here one night, and the atmosphere was electric—everyone was dancing, singing along, and having a great time. It's the type of place where you can completely unwind and have a good time.

If you're looking for something more private, visit El Cercle, a modest cultural center in the heart of the Old Town. This facility features a wide range of live acts, from acoustic sets to poetry readings, and the atmosphere is always comfortable and inclusive. I stumbled upon an acoustic folk duo performing here one evening and felt as if I was attending a private concert. The crowd was tiny, but the energy in the room was warm and welcoming—a fitting finale to a relaxed evening.

Best Places for Late-Night Snacks

Let's be honest: No night out is complete without a late-night snack. Girona also has some great choices for those post-bar hunger. Whether you're craving a hefty sandwich or a sweet dessert, the city has got you covered.

Café Le Bistrot, a charming small café in the Old Town that serves wonderful crepes late into the night, was one of my favorites. After a few cocktails, nothing beats sinking your teeth into a warm, buttery crepe stuffed with Nutella and bananas. It's the kind of indulgence that makes you feel like a kid again, and I might have returned more times than I like to confess.

For something a little more savory, go to Can Roca 2, a local restaurant known for its bocadillos (Spanish sandwiches). This restaurant stays open late and serves legendary bocadillo de jamón (ham sandwich). It's simple but incredibly fulfilling, especially after a night of dancing or bar hopping. Pair it with a cold beer for the ideal late-night snack.

If you want something more substantial, La Bombonerais is a terrific choice. This restaurant is known for its tapas, and they keep the kitchen open late, so you can get your fill of patatas bravas, calamari, and croquetas even after the bars close. I made the mistake of ordering a little bit of everything one night, which resulted in a wonderful tapas coma—but let me tell you, every mouthful was worth it.

Nightlife Etiquette in Girona

Before you go out, you should be aware with Girona's nighttime etiquette. For starters, the locals tend to stay out late—really late. Dinner frequently doesn't begin until 9 or 10 p.m., so most people don't visit the bars until at least 11 p.m., and the clubs don't really get going until beyond midnight. So, if you're used to starting your night out early, you might want to change your plans (or take a siesta) to truly enjoy Girona's nightlife.

Another thing to keep in mind is that Girona's nightlife is often more relaxed than in other larger cities. People here are pleasant and gregarious, although the atmosphere is more relaxed and casual. Don't be shocked if you strike up a discussion with the bartender or make new acquaintances at a nearby table—Girona's nightlife revolves around good company, music, and beverages.

Finally, tipping is less common in Spain than in other countries. However, leaving a little tip—especially if you have had excellent service—is always appreciated.

Girona at night is a magnificent experience, with something for everyone, whether you want to dance the night away, take a peaceful promenade, or drink cocktails under the stars. The city's appeal does not vanish with the light of day; rather, it intensifies, exposing a whole new side to this exquisite corner of Catalonia. So, whether you're a night owl or prefer to relax in the evening, Girona has a night out for you. Just be prepared to fall even more in love with the city as the sun goes down.

Chapter 11

FESTIVALS AND EVENTS IN GIRONA

Girona is a city that enjoys celebrating. Whatever the season, there's always something going on, whether it's a brilliant flower festival, a bustling local fair, or an international cinema week featuring the world's top films. And, believe me, I've traveled to a lot of places, but there's something about Girona's festivals and events that feels unusually intimate, almost as if you're being invited into a local secret that the entire city has kept. The air appears to hum with excitement, and every street corner changes into a little stage where locals and visitors alike gather to eat, drink, dance, and celebrate the finest of Catalonian culture.

During my time in Girona, I made sure to immerse myself in the city's event calendar. Whether you schedule your trip around one of Girona's famed festivals or simply happen to come across a local celebration, you're in for a treat. So let me walk you through some of the most memorable festivals and events on the Girona calendar.

Temps de Flors, Girona's Flower Festival

If one event defines Girona's celebratory atmosphere, it's Temps de Flors, the city's world-renowned flower festival. Every May, Girona transforms into a floral utopia, and it's a sight to behold. For one glorious week, the entire city explodes with color as flower displays take over the streets, plazas, and even some of the most renowned buildings. Imagine traveling down a narrow, cobblestone lane, only to round a corner and be met with a gigantic flower installation right out of a storybook.

My first vacation to Girona coincided with Temps de Flors, and it felt like I had stepped into a dream. Flowers were everywhere I looked—cascading down from balconies, fashioned into complex sculptures, and springing from the city walls' gaps. The flower designers' ingenuity is absolutely impressive. One of my favorite exhibits was in the Arab Baths, where they transformed the ancient stone baths into a wonderful oasis, with hundreds of flowers floating on the water's surface. The contrast between the old, aged stone and the new, brilliant flowers was stunning.

But it's not all about flowers. Temps de Flors is a festival of art and community. The streets are alive with live music, pop-up food booths, and art exhibits that encourage you to stay and take in the mood. I recall coming across a jazz band playing in one of the squares, the sound of the saxophone bouncing off the stone walls and the perfume of roses filling the air. It was one of those moments when you pause and wonder, "Is this real life?""

If you enjoy photography, Temps de Flors is the ideal time to visit Girona. Every aspect of the city transforms into an Instagram-worthy backdrop, and you'll find yourself shooting away, trying to capture the beauty of everything. Just make sure you bring a good camera—or at least a phone with plenty of storage space—because you'll need it.

Girona's Sant Narcís Fair

While Temps de Flors focuses on flowers and beauty, Girona's Sant Narcís Fair is where the city truly lets loose. The annual celebration of Girona's patron saint, Sant Narcís, takes place in October and is the city's most popular event. And let me tell you, it's a blast. Consider it a cross between a county fair, a medieval festival, and a city-wide celebration that lasts more than a week.

The centerpiece of the Sant Narcís Fair is La Devesa Park, which is transformed into a vast fairground with rides, games, and food vendors. I spent the entire afternoon here, channeling my inner child by riding the Ferris wheel, playing carnival games, and eating my weight in churros. The scent of fried dough and the sound of laughing bring out your fun side, regardless of your age.

However, the Sant Narcís Fair offers more than just rides. The entire city participates, including music, parades, and traditional castellers (human tower) acts. Watching the castellers is a unique experience. You stand there, holding your breath, as people— normal individuals, mind you—climb on top of one another to construct a human tower that appears unimaginably tall. And when the smallest member of the group, usually a child, scrambles to the top and raises their hand in triumph, the entire audience goes crazy. It's one of those "only in Catalonia" experiences that will stick with you long after the festival is over.

The correfoc, or fire run, is exciting but often little terrifying. Consider this scenario: it's evening, the streets are crowded, and suddenly, a parade of "devils" equipped with sparklers and pyrotechnics bursts through the throng. The air is thick with the smell of gunpowder, the crackling of fireworks, and people's delighted yells as they dodge the sparks. I may or may not have been singed by a rogue firecracker, but that's all part of the excitement. If you ever get the opportunity to witness a correfoc, take it—you won't regret it.

Film Festivals and Cultural Week

If you enjoy movies like I do, Girona's film festivals and cultural weeks are a must-see. The city has a variety of these events throughout the year, but one of the most notable is the Girona Film Festival, which features independent films from across the world. The festival takes place every September, and it's an excellent opportunity to view some fantastic films that you might not see otherwise.

I went to a few movies throughout the festival, and what struck me was the small setting. Unlike large film festivals, where you feel like just another face in a crowd, the Girona Film Festival is intimate and warm. You can actually speak with the directors, attend Q&A sessions, and gain a better understanding of the creative process behind the films. Furthermore, the locations are stunning—there's something amazing about viewing a movie at a medieval theater in the heart of Girona.

In addition to the film festival, Girona offers a variety of cultural weeks throughout the year, each focusing on a particular aspect of Catalan culture. Throughout these weeks, the city is alive with seminars, talks, and performances celebrating everything from literature to gastronomy. I was fortunate enough to be in town during Catalan Book Week, and I spent the entire afternoon walking through book booths, meeting with local writers, and even purchasing a few Catalan novels (which, admittedly, I'm still working my way through with the help of Google Translate).

Sporting Events and Marathons

Girona offers a variety of sporting events and marathons to get your pulse pounding. Girona is well-known for its passion of cycling, and if you enjoy the sport, here is the place to be. Several cycling competitions are held throughout the year, attracting both amateurs and pros, and professional cyclists are frequently seen practicing on the city's roads.

The Girona Gran Fondo, a multi-day event that includes a hard road race, a gravel ride, and even a time trial, is one of the most important cycling events of the year. I'm no professional cyclist, but I did participate in the more informal Gran Fondoride, and let me tell you, it was difficult but extremely satisfying. There's nothing quite like cycling through Girona's beautiful countryside, with the wind in your face and the Pyrenees in the background. And the camaraderie among the cyclists was incredible—everyone was there to have a good time, whatever of skill level.

If cycling isn't your thing, Girona organizes a number of marathons and running events each year. The Girona Marathon, conducted in March, is one of the city's most popular marathons, attracting participants from all over the world. The race takes you through Girona's core, past ancient sites, and out into the countryside. Even if you are not running, it is enjoyable to cheer on the competitors as they sprint through the streets.

Music Festivals & Concerts

Music fans, rejoice—Girona boasts a thriving music scene that comes life during the city's numerous music festivals and performances. The Nits de Clàssicafestival, held in the summer, is a popular event that features classical music concerts at some of Girona's most prominent locales. There's something really magical about listening to a string quartet in the Girona Cathedral cloister, the melodies bouncing off the ancient stone walls as the sun sets behind the spires. I saw one of these concerts, and it was unquestionably one of the most beautiful musical experiences I've ever had.

However, the music scene in Girona is far from limited to classical music. The Strenes Festival, held every spring, celebrates contemporary Catalan and Spanish music with concerts in various venues throughout the city. One of the festival's most distinguishing aspects is its rooftop concerts, which allow you to see some of the region's best musicians perform while perched on top of Girona's skyscrapers. I attended a rooftop concert by a local indie band, and the mix of excellent music, breathtaking scenery, and a fresh breeze made for a wonderful evening.

If you enjoy jazz, make sure to visit Sunset Jazz Club, which I mentioned earlier. The club frequently hosts special events and performances during Girona's music festivals, and it's the ideal location to relax with a glass of wine and some soft melodies.

Seasonal Markets and Craft Fairs

Finally, no vacation to Girona is complete without stopping by one of the city's seasonal markets or craft fairs. These events take place throughout the year, providing anything from local vegetables to homemade crafts, and they're an excellent way to experience Girona's lively community spirit.

One of the best markets is the Christmas Market, which takes over Girona's streets each December. The market is packed with stalls offering everything from Christmas decorations to local foods, and the entire city is lit up in glittering lights. On a chilly evening, I walked through the market, sipping hot mulled wine and munching on roasted chestnuts. It was the ideal way to get into the holiday mood, and I may have gone a bit crazy purchasing handmade decorations to take home.

For something a little different, visit the Medieval Market, which takes place every November. The market is held in Girona's Old Town and transforms the city into a medieval hamlet, complete with costumed entertainers, traditional crafts, and food stalls selling medieval cuisine. I spent hours roaming through the market, observing blacksmiths at work, sipping honeyed mead, and even attempting archery (to varied degrees of success).

Girona's festivals and events provide insight into the city's heart and spirit. Girona is known for its celebrations, whether it's during Temps de Flors, Sant Narcís Fair, or local markets. The city's festivals are more than just events; they provide an opportunity to connect with the local culture, meet new people, and experience the joy and love that make Girona so special. So, anytime you visit Girona, make sure to see what's going on—you never know what kind of magic the city has in store.

Chapter 12

FAMILY-FRIENDLY ACTIVITIES IN GIRONA

Girona is a city that captivates visitors of all ages. Whether you are a lone traveler, a couple on a romantic holiday, or a family with active children, there is always something to keep everyone entertained. To be honest, as someone who prefers solo trips and long hikes through medieval towns, I was surprised to discover Girona's family-friendliness. But after spending time with a friend's family during one of my visits, I realized that this city is full of things that are great for kids—and also fun for adults.

Girona has a variety of activities for children, ranging from kid-friendly museums to big parks, while parents can enjoy the city's beauty and culture. And the best part? Exploring Girona with the family never feels like a chore. Everything is accessible, walkable, and full of opportunity for unexpected discoveries. Let's take a look at some of Girona's best family-friendly activities, as well as some advice for keeping both kids and parents entertained throughout the day.

Best Places to Visit With Kids

When it comes to touring Girona with kids, the city's historical landmarks provide more than just architectural lessons—they're also perfect for adventure. As we made our way up to the Girona Cathedral, I remember seeing my friend's children's eyes light up. Yes, the 90-something steps leading up to the entryway may appear to be a workout (and they are), but for children, it is similar to climbing a medieval stronghold. The parents were astonished by the cathedral's grandeur, but the children were more interested in the fact that it had survived numerous sieges and conflicts. We also pretended to be medieval knights scaling the stone steps, making the climb less intimidating for the children.

The Passeig de la Muralla, the historic city walls that surround the Old Town, is an absolute must-see for families visiting Girona. For adults, it provides amazing panoramic views of the city, while for children, it is like to exploring a big outdoor adventure playground. Walking around the walls, seeing through the thin arrow slits, and envisioning life as a soldier guarding the city is an excellent way to keep young minds entertained while learning about history. There are also other places along the wall where you may take a food break (because, let's be honest, kids are always hungry).

Plaça de la Independència, Girona's main square, is also a good choice for families. Surrounded by cafés and restaurants, it's an ideal spot for parents to have a coffee while their children play in the open space. I've seen several families spread out on the benches, letting their children play and having some downtime. It's one of those places where you can feel the pulse of Girona while still allowing the kids to explore freely.

Girona's Child-Friendly Museums

Girona's museums may not appear to be the most obvious places to take children, but the city contains a surprising amount of exhibitions and hands-on activities that are ideal for inquisitive young minds. I am not exaggerating when I say that I noticed more youngsters than adults during my visit to the Museum of Cinema (Museu del Cinema), and with good reason. This museum is a fantastic location for both children and adults, transporting you through the history of cinema with interactive displays and devices that make learning enjoyable.

The museum's collection ranges from early optical toys to historic film equipment, and there are several possibilities for children to interact with the displays. My friend's children spent hours playing with the zoetropes (early machines that generate moving images from a succession of still images), and they were completely captivated by the ancient film projectors. By the conclusion of our tour, I had to virtually drag them out of the museum, which, as any parent will tell you, is a sign of a good day.

Another excellent choice for families is the Girona History Museum. While it may appear dry at first appearance, this museum includes numerous exhibits meant to attract younger visitors. The interactive displays teach children about Girona's rich history, from its Roman origins to the medieval period. One of the attractions for youngsters is a recreation of an old city street, replete with market stalls and cobblestones, which gives them a sense of what life was like in Girona centuries ago. It's instructive without being like "homework," which is always a plus.

If your family enjoys natural history, the Museum of Natural Sciences is another great alternative. It's modest, but the exhibits are interesting for children, featuring displays on local fauna, geology, and fossils. There's even a separate area for younger children to explore, complete with interactive exhibits that teach them about the ecosystem and the creatures that call Catalonia home.

Parks and Playgrounds for Families

Of course, the ideal family activities are those that allow the children to burn off some energy in the great outdoors. Fortunately, Girona offers plenty of parks and playgrounds where families may unwind while the kids play. Parc de la Devesa, which I previously referred to as Girona's "green heart," is one of the city's largest and greatest parks. This vast park is ideal for families, with broad open spaces for children to run around, ride bikes, or kick soccer balls. The towering plane trees provide ample shade, making it a perfect location for a picnic on a sunny day.

The park also offers a designated playground area where children can climb, swing, and slide to their hearts' content. I noted that the playground equipment here is built to accommodate both toddlers and older children, so there is something for everyone. While the kids play, parents can relax on a bench with a book or take a stroll through the park's lovely flowers.

Parc del Migdia, a smaller but equally charming alternative to La Devesa, is another excellent choice. The park's pond is popular with children, especially when they can watch the ducks paddle around. There is also a playground, and the entire park exudes a calm, local air that makes it feel like a hidden treasure. It's the type of spot where families can spend a lazy afternoon, taking in the fresh air and simply enjoying being outside.

For families with older children who enjoy adventure, the Bosc de Can Ginebredanear Banyoles is an excellent day excursion. This one-of-a-kind sculpture park is nestled in a woodland, and while the art is intriguing for adults, children will enjoy the fact that it feels like a gigantic outdoor scavenger hunt. You can walk through the woods and discover unique and often comical sculptures concealed among the trees. It's part art display, part nature hike, and it's popular with families seeking for something unique.

Day Trips Suitable for Children

Girona's central location makes it an ideal base for family-friendly day trips, and there are numerous attractions around that will keep children entertained while parents can explore. One of the best day trips from Girona is to the Costa Brava, where the beautiful beaches and crystal-clear waters will delight the entire family. The coastal communities of Tossa de Mar and Llafrancare are especially appealing to families, with calm waters ideal for swimming and snorkeling.

I'll never forget the sight on my friend's children's faces when they first saw the water in Tossa de Mar. It seemed as if they had stepped into a postcard, with the historic castle on the hill, soft golden sand, and beautiful blue water extending out in front of them. We spent the entire day making sandcastles, collecting seashells, and splashing in the surf. The children enjoyed the freedom of running along the beach, and their parents appreciated the idea that they could relax with a refreshing drink while keeping an eye on them.

For an entirely different experience, visit Banyoles Lake, which is only a short drive from Girona. This beautiful freshwater lake is ideal for a family outing, with plenty of activities to keep everyone entertained. You can rent paddleboats or kayaks to spend the day exploring the lake, or simply rest on the grassy banks while your children swim in the shallow waters. There's also a pleasant walking trail that encircle the lake, ideal for a family stroll or bike trip. We had a relaxing afternoon here, sitting by the water and watching ducks and geese pass by.

If your family prefers animals over beaches, a visit to the Zoo del Pirineu in the neighboring Pyrenees is a must. This small, family-run zoo concentrates on Pyrenees animals and provides an excellent educational experience for children. The children enjoyed getting up close and personal with the animals, especially during the interactive bird of prey performance, which allowed them to see eagles and falcons in action. It's a bit of a journey from Girona, but the breathtaking mountain scenery and opportunity to learn about local fauna make it well worth the trip.

Girona Waterparks and Aquatic Activities

If there is one thing that children can never have enough of, it is water. Fortunately, Girona has several excellent water adventure options that will keep the entire family cool and entertained, especially during the hot summer months.

One of the greatest places to take kids for a day of water fun is Aquadiver, a massive waterpark near Platja d'Aroon on the Costa Brava. This location is packed with water slides, wave pools, and lazy rivers, making it ideal for a family day out. The park is constructed with all ages in mind, so whether you have a child who wants to splash in the little pools or a thrill-seeking teen who wants to take on the park's largest slides, there's something for everyone.

I still laugh when I remember my attempt to race my friend's kids down the Kamikazeslide, one of the park's steepest and fastest rides. Spoiler alert: I lost by a mile. But it was all in good fun, and after a few more rounds of zooming down the slides, we were all floating gently along the Rio Rápido, allowing the current to take us along while we soaked up the sun.

For a more natural water activity, Girona's rivers provide numerous chances for kayaking, paddleboarding, and swimming. The River Ter, which passes through Girona, is ideal for family kayaking trips. Several firms provide kayak rentals and guided trips, and the tranquil waters provide for a safe and fun experience for children. I went on a family-friendly kayaking excursion, and it was such a relaxing way to discover Girona's natural beauties. The children enjoyed kayaking down the river, spotting fish and birds along the way, while the adults relished the opportunity to unwind and take in the landscape.

Family-Friendly Restaurants and Cafés

After a long day of exploring, you'll need somewhere to refuel. Fortunately, Girona boasts a plethora of family-friendly restaurants and cafés that welcome children with open arms—and plenty of high chairs.

Bubbles Gastrobar, a charming restaurant near Plaça de la Independència, is an excellent choice for families. The menu here is full of kid-friendly options, ranging from exquisite pizzas to tasty tapas, and the relaxed environment makes it ideal for parents to unwind while their children eat. I adored their patatas bravas (crispy fried potatoes with spicy sauce), and the kids couldn't get enough of the croquetas. The staff is extremely pleasant and accommodating, ensuring that even the pickiest eaters depart with satisfied bellies.

For a more relaxed meal, La Vienesa is an excellent alternative. This family-friendly café is popular for its wonderful pastries and sandwiches, and it's ideal for a quick lunch or snack. The outside seating area is great for families, with lots of room for children to run around while parents have a cappuccino or a refreshing beverage.

If you're searching for a sweet treat, visit Rocambolesc, an ice cream business managed by the Roca brothers (yep, the same culinary geniuses who created the world-famous El Celler de Can Roca). The ice cream here is incredible, with flavors like caramelized apple and cotton candy that will make both children and adults feel as if they've entered a fantastical dessert fantasy. I had a hard time deciding between all of the scrumptious alternatives, but in the end, I chose the chocolate and olive oil swirl, which was an unexpected but delightful combination.

Girona is a city that seamlessly combines history, culture, and family fun, making it an ideal trip for families. There is never a dull moment, whether it's touring historic city walls or splashing around at water parks. What is the best part? Whatever activity you select, Girona's laid-back attitude allows everyone—young and old—to unwind and enjoy the journey. So pack your luggage, bring your curiosity, and prepare to create amazing family experiences in this quaint Catalan city.

Chapter 13

RELIGIOUS AND SPIRITUAL SITES OF GIRONA

Girona is a city that seamlessly mixes the sacred with the daily. Walking through its streets, you can practically feel the weight of history beneath your feet—this medieval town has been shaped by centuries of religion, devotion, and tradition. In my travels, I've seen many of churches, monasteries, and temples, but the spiritual sites in Girona are particularly compelling. Whether it's the sheer scale of its cathedral, the tranquility of its monasteries, or the subtle echoes of its Jewish background, Girona urges you to take a deep breath and immerse yourself in the spiritual riches that surround you.

You don't have to be religious to enjoy these sites. The craftsmanship, architecture, and history inscribed in the walls of Girona's spiritual landmarks are breathtaking. And, let's be honest, standing in a centuries-old church might be the perfect excuse to slow down, ponder, and get away from the pace and bustle of modern life. So let's take a tour of Girona's most fascinating religious and spiritual sites, where history and faith intersect in the most beautiful manner.

Girona Cathedral: A Majestic Symbol

The Girona Cathedral is one of Girona's most prominent landmarks, towering literally over the rest of the city. Perched on a hill overlooking the city, this towering structure is unmistakable with its large stone façade and magnificent stairway leading up to the door. I'll face it: the first time I stood at the base of those 90-something steps, I had to mentally prepare myself for the climb. But once you reach the summit, the effort is completely worthwhile.

The Girona Cathedral is a beautiful blend of architectural styles, including Romanesque, Gothic, and Baroque, giving it a distinct eclectic flavor. Walking inside is like entering another universe, where time slows and you are surrounded by the chilly, echoing calm of centuries-old stone walls. The cathedral's most prominent feature is its huge nave, which is the largest Gothic nave in the world. Standing in the middle of it, looking up at the towering vaulted ceiling, I couldn't help but feel awestruck. It's one of those locations that makes you feel little, but in the greatest way.

Another must-see is the Cathedral Museum's Tapestry of Creation, a beautiful 11th-century cloth. This finely woven tapestry depicts Biblical subjects and is regarded as one of Europe's most significant pieces of medieval art. As someone who knows almost nothing about tapestry (except for the time I tried knitting and ended up with a crappy potholder), I was astounded by the level of detail and craftsmanship that went into this creation.

Of course, no visit to Girona Cathedral is complete without exploring the Cloister, a calm area enclosed by Romanesque arches and columns. The solitude of the Cloister is a pleasant respite from the cathedral's grandeur, providing a period of thought and peace. I spent a significant amount of time here, simply sitting on one of the stone benches, letting the sunlight bounce off the ancient carvings and picturing what life must have been like for the monks who once roamed these corridors.

Saint Pere de Galligants Monastery

The Sant Pere de Galligants Monastery, a stunning specimen of Romanesque architecture from the 12th century, is located near the cathedral. The monastery today houses Catalonia's Archaeology Museum, but even if you're not interested in archaeology (who doesn't like a nice old pottery shard?), the monastery itself is worth a visit.

Walking into the Sant Pere de Galligants Monastery seems like entering a time capsule. The high, vaulted ceilings and strong stone walls lend the space a sense of permanence and peace that is difficult to find in modern architecture. The cloister is one of the monastery's most notable features, with beautifully carved capitals showing themes from both the Bible and everyday medieval life. I spent some time studying the carvings, attempting to comprehend the stories they told—there's something immensely fulfilling about discovering the small nuances that sometimes go overlooked.

For those interested in Girona's history, the museum provides an intriguing view into the region's past, with relics dating from prehistoric times to the Middle Ages. Even if you don't go into the museum, merely walking around the monastery and taking in the peaceful ambiance is an experience in itself. I find the simplicity of Romanesque architecture quite calming—it's as if the building itself is a meditation on the passage of time.---

Església de Sant Feliu: Girona's Oldest Church

While the Girona Cathedral frequently gets all the attention, the Església de Sant Feliu deserves just as much. As Girona's oldest church, it has a long history dating back to the early Christian period, and its blend of Romanesque, Gothic, and Baroque components makes it an intriguing study in architectural evolution. Furthermore, it is not every day that you have the opportunity to visit a church that holds the remains of a dragon-slaying saint. Yes, you read it correctly.

Saint Felix, or Sant Feliu, is Girona's patron saint, and tradition has it that he fought a dragon—an image you'll see displayed throughout the chapel. The church is notably noted for its collection of paleochristian sarcophagi, which are on exhibit beside the altar. These beautifully carved tombs, dating back to the fourth century, serve as a compelling reminder of Girona's rich and varied history.

Climbing the bell tower of Sant Feliu is an adventure in itself. The tower provides some of the best views of Girona, and as you ascend the winding stone staircase, you can practically hear the echoes of centuries of church bells booming around the city. The view from the summit is breathtaking, especially around sunset, when the golden light casts a warm glow over the city

.

Sant Daniel Monastery: Peace and Serenity

If you want to escape the city's hustle and bustle, the Sant Daniel Monastery is the ideal destination to discover peace and quiet. This centuries-old Benedictine abbey, nestled in a lovely valley just outside Girona, seems to be in another universe. The winding road leading to the monastery is bordered with trees, and when you arrive, you'll feel as if you've entered a peaceful, rural refuge.

The Sant Daniel Monastery is still home to a small community of nuns, giving it a distinct sense of living history. The monastery's simple, graceful architecture symbolizes Benedictine values of humility and devotion, while the surrounding grounds contribute to a sense of tranquillity. I found myself slowing down as I strolled past the monastery's courtyard, inhaling the aroma of rosemary and lavender that floated through the air.

While the monastery is a serene retreat, it also serves as an excellent starting point for walks in the surrounding area. The Sant Daniel Valley is crisscrossed by walking routes that go through woodlands, across streams, and up into the hills, providing spectacular views of Girona from above. After seeing the monastery, I went for a leisurely climb, and there's nothing quite like being on top of a hill, gazing out over the city, with only the sound of birds and the rustle of leaves in the breeze.

Jewish Heritage Sites and Synagogues

One of the most intriguing parts of Girona's history is its Jewish roots. The city's Jewish Quarter, known as the Call Jueu, is one of the best-preserved in Europe, and wandering through its small, winding lanes is like stepping back in time. Girona had a strong Jewish community during the Middle Ages, and while much of that history was lost after Jews were expelled from Spain in 1492, the Call Jeu still has a palpable feeling of the past.

The Museum of Jewish History is located in the center of the Jewish Quarter and is housed in a refurbished synagogue. The museum depicts the story of Girona's Jewish population, from its origins in the ninth century to its eventual deportation. The exhibitions are both touching and instructive, and I found myself drawn to the human stories of the families who formerly called Girona home.

One of the most outstanding aspects of the Call Jeu is its labyrinthine layout. The streets are small and steep, with stone structures that appear to surround you on all sides. It's easy to get lost, but that's part of the appeal—every turn exposes something new, whether it's a secret courtyard or a centuries-old gateway. Walking around the Call Jeu, you can't help but envision what life was like for the Jewish families who previously called this place home, and the sense of history is nearly overwhelming.

Religious Festivals and Traditions

Girona's religious festivals are an important part of the city's cultural fabric, and even if you aren't religious, they provide an interesting peek into local traditions.

The Feast of Sant Narcís, held annually in October to honor the city's patron saint, is a significant religious celebration in Girona. The celebration is a colorful affair, with parades, fireworks, and the famed correfoc (fire run), but it also has solemn religious processions that wind through the streets, accompanied by the mournful sound of drums and chants.

During Holy Week (Semana Santa), Girona comes alive with religious processions reenacting Christ's Passion. The Holy Burial Procession, held on Good Friday, is one of the most touching processions. The streets of the Old Town are lined with hooded penitents carrying statues of the Virgin Mary and Christ, accompanied by the slow tolling of bells. Watching the procession, with flickering lighting casting long shadows on the stone walls, I couldn't help but feel reverence and amazement. Even though you're only a visitor, it's one of those moments when you feel strongly connected to the place's history and customs.

Another noteworthy custom is the Catalan pilgrimage to the Sant Miquel del Faimonastery in the surrounding mountains. This annual pilgrimage attracts locals from all around the region, who walk to the isolated monastery. The pilgrimage is a religious and social occasion, with families, friends, and even strangers gathering to enjoy the experience. It serves as a reminder that for many Gironians, religion is more than simply a personal belief; it is also a social celebration.

Girona's religious and spiritual sites are more than just landmarks; they are living reminders of the city's history, culture, and faith. Whether you're standing in awe at the Girona Cathedral's towering nave, seeking serenity in the tranquility of the Sant Daniel Monastery, or walking the narrow alleyways of the Call Jueu, Girona's spiritual legacy has something for everyone. The city begs you to slow down, contemplate, and learn about the stories that have shaped it throughout the centuries. And who knows. You might even leave with a newfound appreciation for the world around you—just be prepared to be awed by the sheer beauty of it all.

Chapter 14

ACCOMMODATION IN GIRONA

Girona provides many of possibilities for finding the ideal location to stay. Whether you're searching for a five-star experience with all the trappings, a quaint boutique guesthouse in the center of the Old Town, or a quirky and unusual accommodation that will make your vacation unforgettable, this city has you covered. During my visits, I tried a range of lodging choices, and let me tell you, each one added a unique flavor to my time in Girona.

Girona's appeal stems from its ability to accommodate various types of travelers. The city has a laid-back attitude, so wherever you stay, you'll feel like you're part of the beat. One minute you're relaxing by a rooftop pool with a glass of cava, and the next you're meeting a local guesthouse owner who insists on sharing his family's secret churro recipe with you. Every type of visitor will find something here, whether you're a solitary backpacker on a tight budget, a couple looking for a romantic break, or a family seeking comfort and convenience. So, let's have a look at Girona's hotel options and choose the best locations to stay after a day of touring this lovely city.

Overview of Accommodation Options

Girona has a wide choice of hotel options to suit every preference and budget. There are plenty of fantastic places to stay, ranging from high-end luxury hotels with panoramic city views to mid-range hotels that strike a mix between comfort and price. You'll also discover lots of boutique guesthouses, one-of-a-kind stays in ancient buildings, and accommodations conveniently located near Girona's Old Town, providing easy access to all of the city's major attractions.

But it's more than just where you sleep; it's also about how your accommodations improve your experience. Staying in the Old Town immerses you in the city's historic beauty, whereas a luxury resort on the outskirts provides a tranquil escape with all the bells and whistles. Or, if you're like me and enjoy a nice eccentric experience, Girona has some one-of-a-kind accommodations that will make your vacation memorable for years. Let's look at the various types of accommodations and what you can expect from them.

Luxury Hotels and Resorts

Girona boasts various luxury hotels and resorts that offer style, comfort, and service. These lodgings frequently include rooftop pools, gourmet restaurants, and spa services—ideal for unwinding after a full day of touring.

The Hotel Carlemany Girona, located on Plaça Miquel Santaló, is one of Girona's most luxurious hotels. This four-star hotel blends modern elegance with great service, and its central location allows you easy access to both the Old Town and the city's newer areas. The rooms are big, with luxurious beds and a contemporary décor. What truly won me on this hotel was the Indigo Restaurant & Lounge, which serves a contemporary take on traditional Catalan food. Additionally, the outdoor patio is ideal for drinking a cocktail in the evening.

Hotel Nord 1901 Superior, located at Carrer Nord, 7-9, provides an even more upmarket experience with a boutique luxury ambiance. This location is an absolute hidden gem, tucked away on a quiet street but only a few minutes from the Old Town. What I liked best about Hotel Nord 1901 was the rooftop pool. On a hot summer day, nothing beats taking a plunge while admiring the city's panoramic vistas. The accommodations are modern but warm, and the staff goes out of their way to make you feel right at home.

If you want to have a full resort experience just outside the city, Mas de Torrent Hotel & Spa is the place to go. This five-star hotel, located in the adjacent Costa Brava region, has breathtaking views, elegant accommodations, and a world-renowned spa. It's approximately a 30-minute drive from Girona, but the trip is well worth it if you want to unwind and be pampered. The hotel is located in a restored 18th-century Catalan farmhouse, and the combination of classic architecture and modern comfort is just beautiful.

Mid-range Hotels for Comfort

If you want to combine comfort and budget, Girona has a superb selection of mid-range hotels that do not sacrifice on decor or services. These hotels provide all of the essentials—comfortable rooms, convenient locations, and friendly staff—without breaking the bank.

Hotel Gran Ultonia, located at Gran Via de Jaume I, 22, is one of my favorite midrange options. This hotel is in an excellent location, only a short walk from Girona Cathedral and the Old Town. The rooms are clean, modern, and spacious, and come equipped with everything you need for a comfortable stay. What distinguishes Hotel Gran Ultonia is its rooftop terrace, which provides stunning views of the city. I spent many hours up there with a bottle of wine, admiring the sunset over Girona's skyline.

Peninsular Hotel, located in Carrer Nou 3, has a bit more boutique vibe. This hotel is an excellent mid-range choice with a touch of historical charm. The building itself dates back to the nineteenth century, and while the rooms have been modernized, they nevertheless offer an air of old-world elegance. The location is great, in the middle of Girona, and the staff is quite friendly. Furthermore, the breakfast here is fantastic—lots of fresh pastries, fruit, and, of course, strong Catalan coffee.

Another excellent mid-range option is Ciutat de Girona, located at Carrer Nord, 2. This hotel boasts a beautiful, contemporary style and provides excellent service. The rooms are spacious and pleasant, and the location couldn't be better—right next to the Pont de Pedra, one of Girona's most historic bridges. One thing I liked about Ciutat de Girona is its emphasis on sustainability, with eco-friendly procedures throughout the hotel.

Unique Stays

If you're like me and enjoy staying somewhere out of the ordinary, Girona has plenty of unusual hotel options to make your trip even more memorable. Whether it's a quirky Airbnb or a restored historic structure, these accommodations provide a unique alternative to the traditional hotel experience.

Casa Cundaro, on Carrer de la Força 15, was one of the most interesting locations I stayed in Girona. This guesthouse is located in a 15th-century structure in the heart of the Call Jueu (Jewish Quarter), and staying here feels like stepping back in time. The rooms are furnished with old furniture and original stone walls, giving the property a warm, historic atmosphere. The building is part of the Museum of Jewish History, so you'll be staying in a piece of Girona's rich history. I enjoyed strolling the small, labyrinthine streets of the Jewish Quarter after dark, feeling as if I was discovering hidden secrets around every corner.

For something truly unique, visit The Blooming House, which is located just outside Girona in the small village of La Pera. This is an artist's home, complete with unique artwork, vibrant furnishings, and lush gardens. The mansion is a work of art, with sculptures and murals on nearly every surface. Staying here felt like living in a Bohemian fantasy— each room is distinct, and the garden is breathtaking. If you're the type of traveler who enjoys discovering the unusual and fantastic, this is the spot for you.

Staying Near Girona's Old Town

If you want to be in the heart of Girona, staying near the Old Town is a no-brainer. This district is rich in history, charm, and small cobblestone streets, and it is conveniently located within walking distance of all the major attractions. The Old Town is where Girona's soul resides, and staying here allows you to fully immerse yourself in the city's medieval charm.

One of the nicest locations to stay in the Old Town is Hotel Historic, which is located at Carrer Bellmirall 4. This hotel is housed in a wonderfully renovated medieval building with exposed stone walls, wooden beams, and tasteful decor. The rooms are spacious and comfortable, with a blend of modern amenities and historical charm. I enjoyed getting up in the morning, leaving my accommodation, and strolling down the small streets past centuries-old buildings to get a coffee at a neighboring cafe. It's an excellent location for exploring Girona Cathedral, Passeig de la Muralla, and the remainder of the Old Town.

Another excellent alternative is Hotel Museu Llegendes de Girona, located at Carrer Portal de la Barca, 4. As the name implies, this hotel is dedicated to Girona's mythology and folklore, and the decor reflects that. Each room is styled after a different mythology, lending the hotel a quirky and slightly mysterious atmosphere. The hotel is conveniently located just steps from Girona Cathedral, and guests can enjoy guided excursions of the city's tales. I have to say that sleeping in a room designed after Girona's dragon-slaying legend provided a magical element to my trip.

Boutique Guesthouses

Girona's boutique guesthouses are a pleasant alternative to larger hotels for those seeking a more intimate, personal experience. These smaller hotels frequently offer a more personalized experience, with hosts ready to share their passion of the area and provide insider information.

Casa Migdia is one of my favorite boutique guesthouses in Girona, located in the surrounding village of Sant Jordi Desvalls, just a short drive away. This delightful guesthouse is maintained by a French couple who have converted an old village house into a warm and inviting hideaway. The rooms are well designed, with vintage furniture and creative accents throughout. What I liked best about Casa Migdiawas the genuine hospitality—every morning, the owners would make a delicious breakfast, replete with homemade pastries and fresh orange juice, and sit with the guests to discuss the day's plans.

Bed & Breakfast Bells Oficis is another great boutique choice in Girona, located at Gran Via de Jaume I, 22. This guesthouse is located in a stunning ancient structure, and the rooms are modest yet lovely, with high ceilings and huge windows that let in lots of natural light. Joan, the owner, is exceedingly nice and goes out of his way to make people feel at home. It's the type of place where you feel more like you're staying with friends than in a hotel, and the location is ideal—just a short walk from Girona Cathedral and the Onyar River.

Top Recommended Hotels and Resorts

After sampling various lodgings in Girona, a couple stand out to me as high recommendations for different sorts of travelers:

- Hotel Nord 1901 Superior is ideal for anyone seeking a boutique luxury experience in the center of Girona. The rooftop pool and central location make it an excellent choice.

- Peninsular Hotel: A mid-range hotel with historic appeal, excellent for guests seeking comfort without indulging in luxury.

- Casa Cundaro: Ideal for history aficionados and anyone seeking a distinctive, evocative stay in the Jewish Quarter.

- Mas de Torrent Hotel & Spa: For those looking to pamper themselves to a magnificent countryside getaway just outside of the city.

Choosing the Right Accommodation for You

Choosing the perfect Girona accommodation relies on the type of experience you seek. If you're looking for a romantic retreat, one of the boutique guesthouses or luxury hotels in the Old Town will provide an intimate, delightful experience. Staying at a mid-range hotel with big rooms and a central location allows families to easily explore the city's main attractions. And for those looking for something new, Girona's distinctive accommodations provide a quirky twist that adds an extra element of pleasure to your journey.

When selecting your lodging, consider how much time you'll spend at your hotel versus sightseeing. If you intend to spend the most of your time out and about, a mid-range selection will provide you with adequate comfort without needless frills. However, if you want to rest and be pampered, a luxury stay may be exactly what you need.

Booking Tips to Get the Best Deals

Here are some ideas for getting the greatest deal on lodging in Girona:

- Book early: Girona is a popular tourist destination, especially during events like Temps de Flors. Booking many months in advance gives you more options and lower pricing.

- Travel off-season: Visiting Girona in the spring or fall, outside of the high summer months, can save you money on lodging while still providing pleasant weather.

- Use hotel comparison websites: Websites such as Booking.com and Expedia allow you to compare prices across multiple hotels and frequently provide bargains or discounts.

- Look for package deals: Some hotels provide special packages that include breakfast, guided excursions, or spa treatments, which can increase the value of your stay.

Girona's charm will shine through regardless of where you stay, whether you wake up in a luxury hotel with cathedral views or enjoy coffee on the terrace of a small guesthouse. The city has something for everyone, and the appropriate lodging can elevate a wonderful trip to an outstanding experience. So, select wisely and let Girona to work its magic—after all, a good night's sleep is the best way to prepare for another day of adventure in this stunning city.

Chapter 15

HEALTH AND WELLNESS IN GIRONA

When you think of Girona, the first thing that comes to mind is certainly its medieval beauty, scenic alleyways, and delectable cuisine. But let me tell you, Girona is also an excellent destination to improve your health and wellness. Whether you need some pampering, want to find your zen, or simply need a place to burn off all those tapas, the city has lots of alternatives to keep your body and mind in good form.

Personally, I've always believed that there's no better way to balance off my excessive travel habits than to devote some time to wellness. Girona, with its laid-back vibe and stunning natural surroundings, seems like the ideal spot to refresh. Girona has something for everyone who enjoys wellbeing, from spas and wellness centers to outdoor activities that will make you forget you're exercising. So, let's look at the various methods you may keep your body and mind healthy while enjoying the beauty of this beautiful city.

Spa and Wellness Centers

Let's start with spas, which are perhaps the best component of any wellness routine. There's something irresistibly exquisite about treating yourself to a spa day, and Girona has plenty of options for those in need of some extra care. Whether you're searching for a full-fledged health resort or just a quick massage to relax after a day of sightseeing, there are plenty of options available.

Aqva Gerunda Banys Romans, located in Carrer Ferran el Catòlic 10, is a popular spa destination. This Roman-inspired bathhouse is a true jewel, and entering feels like walking back in time. The baths are intended to resemble authentic Roman thermal baths, having hot, warm, and cold waters to cycle between while you relax. There is also a steam room and a variety of massages and treatments available. I scheduled a massage after trekking the Passeig de la Muralla all day (which my legs were not prepared for), and it was the perfect treatment for my tight muscles. The serene setting, gentle lighting, and calming music made me feel as if I were floating out of there. Plus, you're soaking in a setting inspired by ancient Roman baths. That's only a bonus.

If you want something a little more modern, visit Mas de Torrent Spa, which is located just outside Girona in the Costa Brava region. This luxurious spa, located within the Mas de Torrent Hotel & Spa, offers a variety of services, including hydrotherapy pools and individualized cosmetic treatments. The scenery is breathtaking—imagine yourself lounging by the pool, surrounded by lush gardens, with the rolling hills of the countryside in the background. I spent a beautiful afternoon here, rotating between the sauna, the pool, and the outdoor patio, where I sipped herbal tea and did my hardest to look like someone who "does this all the time." It's the type of place where you can actually rest and forget about your concerns.

Yoga Retreats and Meditation Spots

If you prefer to stretch, breathe, and connect with your inner self (rather than having your back pounded into submission during a massage), Girona offers a variety of yoga and meditation options. The city's serene atmosphere gives it an ideal setting for spiritual and physical self-care.

La Bruguera de Púbol is a prominent yoga retreat center in Girona, situated in the nearby village of Púbol. This facility is a small slice of paradise, nestled in the heart of a natural reserve, with eco-friendly accommodations and a stunning yoga studio that overlooks the green countryside. Whether you're an experienced yogi or a total beginner, these retreats provide an opportunity to unplug from the outer world and focus on your practice. I signed up for a weekend retreat, and it was one of the most revitalizing experiences I've had in recent years. The mix of morning yoga, meditation sessions, and healthy, locally sourced meals made me feel completely transformed. The location is ideal for exploring Gala Dalí Castle, which is only a short walk away.

Yoga Girona, located near the city center, offers daily courses in a quiet, welcoming atmosphere. The studio is located at Carrer Santa Eugènia, 54, and offers a variety of techniques, including Vinyasa, Hatha, and even pregnant yoga. What I like best about Yoga Girona is the sense of community—everyone, from the teachers to the students, is welcoming and friendly, making it an ideal spot for guests to drop in for a class. Furthermore, they provide sessions in both Catalan and English, so you don't have to worry about language difficulties while practicing your downward dog.

If you're searching for a truly calm meditation area, visit Sant Daniel Valley, just outside Girona. The valley is home to the Sant Daniel Monastery, a centuries-old Benedictine monastery that provides one of the most tranquil settings I've ever seen. Walking through the valley, with its flowing streams and lush hills, I experienced an overpowering sensation of tranquility. It's ideal for a calm, self-guided meditation session, with the only sounds being birdsong and the rustling of leaves in the breeze.

Gyms and Fitness Centers in Girona

Girona boasts a selection of gyms and fitness centers where you may work up a sweat for those of us who prefer a more active approach to wellbeing (or who simply need a guilt-free excuse to indulge in more tapas). Whether you prefer weightlifting, spinning classes, or a good old-fashioned treadmill, the city has something to suit your fitness needs.

Holmes Place Girona, located at Carrer de Barcelona 103, is one of the city's top gyms. This fitness center is part of a larger chain, but it has everything you could want in a gym: cutting-edge equipment, a diverse range of training courses, and a sleek, modern setting that feels more like a high-end hotel than a regular gym. I went to a spinning class, and while I will admit that I was gasping for air halfway through, the cheerful music and energetic instructor kept me motivated. After your workout, you may rest in the gym's spa area, which includes a pool, sauna, and steam room.

Another excellent alternative is Dir Girona, which is located at Carrer de l'Agusti Riera i Pau 11. This gym is ideal for individuals seeking a more relaxed, no-frills workout experience. They provide a variety of group fitness courses, such as Zumba, Pilates, and HIIT, as well as plenty of cardio and strength-training equipment. What I liked about Dir Girona was the nice, laid-back vibe—it's the type of gym where everyone seems to know each other, and the atmosphere is quite welcome. Furthermore, they provide flexible membership choices, allowing you to sign up for only a few days or a week if you're visiting the area.

For something unique, visit CrossFit Girona, located in Carrer del Riu Güell, 16. This area is ideal if you enjoy high-intensity, functional exercise and want to get your heart rate up. The teachers here are fantastic—very knowledgable and encouraging—and will make sure you receive a great workout, even if you are new to CrossFit. I joined one of their group courses, and by the end of it, I was pouring with perspiration and feeling like I could take on the world (or at least another plate of patatas bravas).

Girona's Outdoor Wellness Activities

Of course, one of Girona's best features is its natural beauty, which makes it ideal for outdoor wellness activities. Whether you prefer hiking, cycling, or simply taking a tranquil stroll through nature, Girona provides numerous opportunities to stay active while enjoying the great outdoors.

One of my favorite outdoor activities in Girona is trekking the Sant Miqueltrail. The climb begins just outside the city and leads to the Sant Miquel Castle, a ruined medieval fortification with stunning panoramic views of Girona and the surrounding countryside. The trek itself is rather easy, and the trail winds through lush woodlands, providing a tranquil respite from the rush and bustle of the city. I enjoy hiking here in the early morning, when the air is still chilly and the sun shines through the trees. Reaching the top of the hill, looking out over the scenery, and simply breathing it all in seems like the pinnacle of wellness.

If you like to cycle, Girona is a cyclist's heaven. The city is well-known for its bicycle routes, which offer lots of alternatives for both casual and serious riders. A popular option is to ride up to Els Àngels, a hilltop refuge with breathtaking views of the surrounding area. The ride is difficult, with several steep ascents, but the reward at the summit is well worth it. Furthermore, Girona's mild climate makes it ideal for riding year-round, allowing you to get your fitness fix while seeing the stunning Catalan countryside.

For a more relaxed outdoor activity, take a calm walk along the Onyar River's banks. The river runs through the center of Girona, and wandering along its banks is a terrific way to unwind while taking in the surroundings. Several bridges span the river, providing lovely vistas of the colorful buildings that surround the bank. It's an ideal location for a leisurely stroll, especially in the late afternoon when the golden light shines off the ocean.

Where to Find Medical Help and Pharmacies

While I hope you don't need it during your trip, it's always a good idea to know where to obtain medical aid and pharmacies in case you do. Girona has a well-equipped healthcare system, with numerous hospitals, clinics, and pharmacies spread around the city.

If you require medical assistance, the city's major hospital, Hospital Universitari de Girona Doctor Josep Trueta, is located on Av. de França, S/N. The hospital is modern and well-staffed, and the emergency department is open around the clock. I've heard nothing but positive feedback about the quality of care here, and many of the doctors and nurses understand English, which is always a relief when dealing with a medical issue in a foreign country.

Girona has a large number of pharmacies where you may purchase over-the-counter pharmaceuticals, first-aid supplies, and other health-related items. Pharmacies in Spain are marked with a green cross and can be found throughout the city. Farmàcia Francesc Rodríguez is conveniently located in Carrer de l'Argenteria, 7, in the heart of the Old Town. The staff is polite and competent, and they can typically offer assistance or propose a product if you're unsure what you need.

Health Tips for Travelers in Girona

Before you pack your bags and travel to Girona, here are some health considerations to bear in mind:

- Stay hydrated: Girona can get hot in the summer, so bring a water bottle with you, especially if you're spending time outside.

- Wear comfortable shoes: The cobblestone streets of Girona's Old Town are attractive, but they might be difficult to walk on. If you want to do a lot of walking, choose durable, comfy shoes.

- Sunscreen is your friend: Whether you're biking, hiking, or simply wandering around the city, the Spanish sun can be harsh. Even on cloudy days, make sure to apply sunscreen.

- Go easy on the rich food: Catalan cuisine is great, but it can be quite heavy. Balance those rich meals with lighter options such as salads or fresh seafood, and don't be afraid to indulge in moderation.

- Keep local emergency numbers handy: In Spain, the general emergency number is 112, which can be used to contact police, firefighters, or medical personnel.

Staying healthy and feeling good in Girona is simple when you have so many wellness alternatives at your disposal. Whether you're indulging yourself to a spa day, hiking through the countryside, or simply finding tranquility in one of the city's lovely parks, Girona has everything you need to keep your body and mind in tip-top condition. So, the next time you visit, make time for some self-care; you deserve it. After all, what is a holiday without some indulgence and plenty of relaxation?

Chapter 16

WHAT TO DO AND NOT DO IN GIRONA

Traveling to a new location is usually thrilling, but it can also be intimidating when it comes to learning local customs and knowing how to act. Girona, with its rich history, relaxed atmosphere, and welcoming residents, is no exception. However, as with any place, there are some unsaid customs and cultural nuances that you should be aware of before visiting. After spending a large amount of time in Girona, I've learned some tips and methods that will help you avoid unpleasant situations, interact with locals, and genuinely experience the finest that this Catalan gem has to offer.

Let's look at some dos and don'ts to bear in mind while exploring Girona. From comprehending local etiquette to negotiating legal laws, this chapter will walk you through the cultural and practical aspects of this fantastic city. And, of course, I'll throw in some humor along the way—because travel should be enjoyable, even if you're trying to avoid standing out like a sore thumb.

Cultural Etiquette: Respect for Local Customs

Girona, like the rest of Catalonia, has a unique culture, language, and customs that distinguish it from the rest of Spain. While the inhabitants are polite and inviting, they value guests who make an effort to follow their traditions. And believe me, a little cultural sensitivity can go a long way toward making your stay in Girona even more delightful.

Do: Greet them with a smile and "Bon dia" (good morning). People in Girona greet each other warmly, even when passing on the street. A simple "Bon dia" or "Bona tarda" (Good afternoon) may get smiles and perhaps even a polite conversation. You don't have to be fluent in Catalan, but knowing a few fundamental words will help you impress the locals.

Don't: assume everyone speaks Spanish (or English, for that matter). While most people in Girona speak

Spanish, the region's official language is Catalan. Many locals prefer to speak Catalan in their daily lives. If you're not sure which language to speak, start with Catalan greetings; if the conversation moves to Spanish, you'll know you're on the correct route. Just don't expect everyone to react in English—this is still Spain, after all, and it's always welcomed when people try to speak the local language, even if only a few words.

Do: Respect the siesta time. While the siesta custom is not as closely adhered to in Girona as it is in other regions of Spain, many shops, particularly those outside of tourist districts, nevertheless close for a few hours each afternoon. From approximately 1:30 p.m. You can find yourself walking empty streets until 4:30 p.m., wondering where everyone went. Don't worry, it's not you; it's the siesta. This is the ideal time to take a long, leisurely lunch (which is almost a national hobby here).

Don't: rush your meals. Speaking about extended lunches, the idea of dining on the go is nearly sacrilegious in Girona. Meals are designed to be enjoyed, particularly lunch, which is usually the largest meal of the day. When dining out, take your time, enjoy your meal, and embrace the easygoing atmosphere. Don't expect the bill to arrive as soon as you finish your meal—if you're ready to leave, you'll need to request it ("El compte, si nous plau"). All of this is part of the laid-back Catalan lifestyle.

Tourist Tips: How to Behave Like a Local

One of the greatest ways to properly explore Girona is to immerse yourself in the local culture. This not only enriches your experience, but also demonstrates respect for the people who live in this wonderful city. Here are some pointers on how to traverse Girona like a pro.

Do: Participate in the local festivals. Girona is known for its lively events, including the Temps de Florsflower festival and the Sant Narcís Fair. Locals like these activities and are often pleased to see tourists engaging in the excitement. Don't be a passive observer; get engaged! Walk around the flower displays, try your hand at traditional Catalan dancing, or cheer on the human towers during the castellers' performance. These festivals provide an excellent opportunity to immerse yourself in the culture and feel like a member of the community.

Don't: Arrive too early for supper. This is a common error that many tourists make. In Girona, supper does not begin until around 8:30 p.m. (at the very least), and most locals won't have dinner until 9 or 10 p.m. So, say you arrive at a restaurant at 6:30 p.m. If you expect a busy dinner crowd, you will most likely be met with empty tables and confused staff. Take advantage of the local rhythm by getting a pre-dinner drink and some tapas at a bar while you wait for the restaurants to open.

Do: Enjoy the coffee culture. In Girona, coffee is more than just a caffeine fix; it's a ritual. Locals frequently sit for extended periods of time, enjoying their café amb llet (coffee with milk) and chatting up with friends. There's no rush, and the atmosphere is very easygoing. I propose taking a seat in one of the city's picturesque squares, ordering a coffee, and watching the world go by. Just don't expect a large, takeaway-style latte—coffee here is delivered in smaller, stronger amounts and is meant to be enjoyed.

Don't: Forget to attempt vermut (vermouth). While most people connect Spain with wine, Girona boasts a vibrant vermutculture. Locals frequently drink a glass of vermouth as an aperitif before lunch, and it's an excellent way to ease into a lengthy meal. Go to a neighborhood bar, get a glass of vermouth with a slice of orange, and accompany it with some olives or patata bravas. Don't miss out on this adventure.

Common Mistakes to Avoid as a Tourist

As with any destination, there are certain frequent tourist mistakes that can be easily avoided with a little local knowledge. Here are a few things to watch out for in Girona.

Don't: Walk on the bike lanes. Girona is a cyclist's dream, and the city is dotted with bike lanes that crisscross the streets. While it could appear like an enticing spot to walk, especially when the sidewalks grow busy, avoid the desire. Girona's cyclists take their bike lanes seriously. You don't want to be the tourist who causes a near-miss with a professional cyclist during a training ride. Stick to the sidewalks; everyone will be happier for it.

Don't: Wear beachwear in the city. Girona may be near to the Costa Brava, yet it remains a somewhat conservative city in terms of fashion. While it is completely okay to wear a swimsuit to the beach, wandering around town in beachwear (or even flip-flops) is considered bad form. When visiting Girona, dress casually yet smartly—think comfortable, breezy clothes suitable for both sightseeing and a wonderful supper. Also, preserve your beach gear for the actual beach.

Don't: Flash your money. While Girona is a highly safe city, you should still be cautious with your things, especially in crowded areas or tourist sites. Avoid carrying significant quantities of cash, and keep your wallet and phone in safe, closed pockets or backpacks. Pickpocketing can occur in any place, so staying cautious will help guarantee that your trip is stress-free.

Safety Tips for Travelers

Girona is a safe and inviting city, but like with any other place, you should be alert of your surroundings and take a few basic measures. Here's what you need to know about being safe during your vacation.

DO: Be cautious in crowded situations. Places like Girona Cathedral and Plaça de la Independència can get very crowded, especially during festivals or peak tourist seasons. While the city is typically safe, these densely populated locations might be excellent targets for pickpockets. Keep an eye on your valuables and carry a crossbody bag or backpack with a tight zipper.

Don't be careless with your personal possessions. It's never a smart idea to leave your phone, camera, or wallet unattended in public, even for a moment. If you're dining outside at a café, keep your luggage or backpack close by or hook the strap across your chair. This tiny habit can help you avoid any unpleasant surprises.

Do: Use official taxis or ride-hailing apps. If you're going out late at night or traveling alone, it's best to use an official cab or utilize a ridesharing service like Uber. While Girona is a safe city, adopting these steps assures that you are in capable hands. Taxis in Girona are dependable and easy to find—just seek for white vehicles with a green light on top.

Environmental Awareness: Green Travel

Girona has recently taken steps to become a more environmentally friendly city. As a visitor, you can help maintain the city clean and lovely by practicing a few green travel practices.

Do: Bring a reusable water bottle. Girona has various water fountains where you may refill your bottle, so you don't have to keep purchasing single-use plastic bottles. Furthermore, the tap water here is completely safe to drink, allowing you to stay hydrated without contributing to plastic trash.

Don't: Litter. This may appear apparent, but you'd be amazed how frequently I've seen travelers carelessly drop their rubbish on the ground. Girona is a tidy and well-kept city, and its residents take pride in keeping it that way. Make sure to properly dispose of your rubbish, and if you're going for a hike or picnic, pack out what you bring in.

Do: Take public transportation or walk. Girona is a fairly walkable city, and its public transportation system is efficient and user-friendly. If you stay in or near the Old Town, the most of the attractions are easily accessible on foot. Walking is not just good for your health; it also helps to lessen your carbon footprint. Furthermore, meandering around Girona's lovely streets is one of the greatest ways to explore the city.

Legal Regulations: What You Should Know

Finally, let's go over some basic legal restrictions to help you avoid difficulties throughout your time in Girona.

Do: Bring your ID or passport. In Spain, it is mandatory to carry identification at all times. While you're unlikely to be asked for it frequently, it's a good idea to have your passport or a replica on hand, especially if you're renting a car or staying at a hotel.

Don't: Smoke in public areas. Spain has severe anti-smoking legislation, and smoking is not permitted in enclosed public venues such as restaurants, bars, or public transportation. If you smoke, make sure to light up in approved smoking locations, which are normally accessible outside.

Do: Be aware of noise levels. Girona is a relatively tranquil city, particularly in the residential districts. If you're staying in a guesthouse or apartment, respect your neighbors and keep noise to a minimum, especially in the evening. Late-night partying is more common in Barcelona, while Girona tends to keep things quieter.

Keeping these dos and don'ts in mind will not only make your stay in Girona more enjoyable, but will also demonstrate respect for the city and its citizens. It's all about fitting in, appreciating the local culture, and being aware of the little details that make Girona so distinct. So go ahead and tour the city, eat excellent food, and create memories you'll treasure long after your trip is done. Simply remember to say "Bon dia" with a smile, don't rush your meals, and, for the love of all things holy, keep out of the bike lanes!

Chapter 17

GIRONA'S RIVER ONYAR

One of the first things I saw when I arrived in Girona was the River Onyar. It is the city's heart and soul, snaking across the center like a dazzling ribbon, separating the ancient and new. The river has an irresistible allure—like a scene from a storybook—and you immediately realize that it serves as more than just a natural barrier. It's a gathering area, a gorgeous backdrop, and a significant figure in Girona's history. Spending time by the Onyar is nearly unavoidable on any trip to Girona, and why would you want to avoid it? From the renowned bridges to the colorful buildings that line its banks, the river emanates an irresistible charm.

During my time in Girona, I was always drawn back to the river. Whether I was photographing the bright reflections or enjoying a coffee at one of the many riverfront cafés, the Onyar always felt like the ideal companion for my adventures. So, let's take a walk down the river, discover its wonders, and perhaps even dip our toes—metaphorically and literally—into everything it has to offer.

Girona Bridges: Iconic Structures

Girona's bridges are more than simply practical ways to cross the river; they are also renowned icons, each with its own narrative and personality. As you explore the city, you'll cross the Onyar multiple times, and each bridge offers a unique perspective, vista, and slice of Girona's charm.

Let's begin with the most famous of them all: the Pont de les Peixateries Velles. This bright red bridge, created by none other than Gustave Eiffel (yep, the same man who built that massive tower in Paris), is a true showpiece. It was built in 1877, and while it isn't as tall or imposing as its Parisian counterpart, it's nevertheless one of Girona's most popular attractions. Walking across it is like walking through a postcard, with the brilliant hues of the casas de l'Onyar (those renowned riverside mansions) reflected in the water below. On a beautiful day, the bridge's vivid red latticework stands out against the blue sky, and you'll find yourself pausing halfway across to soak in the views. And, of course, take a photo or two—because if you don't Instagram it, did it actually happen?

Another bridge worth crossing is the Pont de Pedra (Stone Bridge). This solid stone building is one of Girona's oldest, and while it lacks the flare of Eiffel's bridge, it more than compensates with its elegance. Locals frequently gather here to chat, stroll, or simply lean over the railing to watch the river pass by. I loved crossing this bridge in the early morning, when the city was still waking up and the sun danced on the river's surface. It's a peaceful, thoughtful spot—ideal for taking a deep breath and appreciating Girona's gentler side.

The Pont de Ferro offers a slightly more modern approach. Unlike the other two, this one is more industrial in style, but don't be fooled—it still has some of the best views of the Old Town and the cathedral towering above. The juxtaposition between the modern lines of the bridge and the medieval architecture in the background creates a fascinating image.

Colorful Houses Along the Onyar

The row of colorful houses that flank Girona's riverbanks is one of the city's most famous sights— and, to be honest, one of the most photographed. These pastel-colored structures, known as casas de l'Onyar, are packed perilously along the river's side, their bright colors reflecting magnificently in the water. It's a sight that appears almost too perfect to be true, as if someone meticulously planned the scenario to ensure that every visitor departs with at least 300 shots of the identical view.

What's remarkable about these homes is that they weren't always so colorful. In fact, they were very dreary until the city decided to give them a colorful facelift in the twentieth century. What was the result? A postcard-perfect stretch of riverfront mansions that appear to have been ripped directly from a painting. Each cottage is painted a different color—soft pinks, yellows, blues, and oranges—and the effect is wonderful, especially when the afternoon sun catches them just right, causing their reflections in the tranquil waters underneath.

I spent a lot of time walking down the river, looking up at the houses and picturing what life must be like inside. Some of the structures are now individual homes, while others house businesses, cafés, and even guesthouses. Their crooked windows and balconies, some of which appear to droop dangerously over the river, have an extraordinarily attractive quality. It's the kind of imperfection that adds to its allure—as if the city is always reminding you that it's been lived in, loved, and filled with tales.

River Walks: Scenic Trails

Walking along the riverbanks is one of the greatest ways to experience the Onyar River. Girona is a beautifully walking city, and the river offers various scenic routes that allow you to enjoy the beauty of the water while exploring the city.

There are trails that run parallel to the river on both sides, providing various vistas depending on where you choose to go. My favorite path was the one from Pont de Pedradown to Pont de Sant Feliu. This stroll passes through some of the most scenic portions of the city, with colorful residences on one side and green hills in the distance on the other. If you're lucky, you might see a few swans or ducks flying smoothly along the river—a quiet reminder that nature is always nearby, even in the middle of the city.

The Passeig de la Devesa, a park along the river immediately outside the Old Town, is a particularly nice site for a river walk. This tree-lined promenade provides a more calm, green atmosphere where you may escape the city's hustle and bustle and relax under the shade of tall plane trees. I enjoyed coming here in the late afternoon, when golden light streamed through the branches and produced dappled shadows on the ground. It's ideal for a relaxing stroll, a morning jog, or perhaps a picnic by the sea.

Those who want to extend their trek might follow the river out of the city and into the surrounding countryside. The Camí del Teris is a popular walking and cycling route that follows the river through farmland, forests, and tiny settlements. It's the ideal approach to see Girona's natural beauty while being connected to the river that flows through it.

Photography Locations along the River

Let's be honest: The River Onyar is a photographer's paradise. Whether you're a professional with a high-end camera or an amateur with a smartphone, the river provides limitless opportunity for great photographs. The colorful residences, renowned bridges, and lake reflections make up a picture-perfect sight.

One of the best photography places in Girona is from the Pont de les Peixateries Velles, where you can catch the iconic vista of the colorful buildings along the river, with the Girona Cathedral and the Basilica of Sant Feliuin in the background. The way the buildings are mirrored in the river gives the photograph an almost perfect symmetry. I spent more time than I'd like to admit standing on this bridge, waiting for the light to hit just right or the clouds to make the perfect dramatic backdrop.

Another wonderful photo location is the Pont de Pedra, which allows you to capture the river, bridges, and Old Town all in one shot. The view from here is especially magnificent at sunrise and dusk, when the light is gentle and warm and the city glows golden. If you're feeling daring, stroll down to the riverbank to capture some great low-angle images that highlight the buildings and bridges.

For a unique perspective, visit the Passeig Arqueològic, a pedestrian path above the city walls above the Old Town. From here, you can see the river, the colorful residences, and the entire city spread out in front of you. It's a bit of a climb up there, but believe me, the view is well worth it.

Riverside Cafés and Restaurants

One of my favorite things to do in Girona was sit by the river with a cup of coffee or a bottle of wine, watching the world pass by. There are several wonderful cafés and restaurants along the river that serve everything from quick espressos to leisurely lunches with a view.

La Terra, located on Plaça de la Independència, is a great place to eat beside the river. This vibrant café has a patio that overlooks the river, making it the ideal place to have a cafè amb lletin in the morning or a glass of vermutin in the afternoon. I spent many afternoons here, drinking my drink and watching the colorful houses' reflections wash across the lake. It's a relaxing place to unwind after a morning of sightseeing, and the people-watching is wonderful.

For something more substantial, visit El Celler de Can Roca, one of Girona's most famous restaurants. While not exactly on the river, it is a short walk away and well worth the detour. The Roca brothers own this Michelin-starred restaurant, which provides an unforgettable culinary experience. I'm not going to lie: dining here is a luxury, but if you're a foodie, it's an experience you won't forget. And after such a dinner, a leisurely stroll along the river is ideal for digestion.

If you want something more casual, Café Le Bistrot is another excellent choice. Located just off the river, this charming café serves a variety of tapas and drinks, and its outside seating area is ideal for taking in the atmosphere of the Old Town. I like coming here in the evening, grabbing a plate of patatas bravas, and seeing the lights reflect on the river as the city gradually turned down for the night.

Water Activities at Onyar

While the River Onyarmay is not as large or wild as some of Spain's other rivers, it does provide a few options for those looking to go closer to the water. If you want to add some adventure to your stay in Girona, there are a few aquatic sports to consider.

Kayaking is one of the most popular activities on the river. Several local firms provide kayak rentals and guided tours along the river and beyond, allowing you to see Girona from a whole different perspective. Paddling along the river, with colorful dwellings sprouting up on either side of you, is a strange sensation. It's tranquil, scenic, and a fantastic opportunity to get some exercise while viewing the city from a different perspective.

If kayaking isn't your thing, you may always try a stand-up paddleboard (SUP) experience. While the Onyar is rather tranquil, navigating the river on a paddleboard is a fun endeavor, and it provides a good vantage point for viewing the city's landmarks. I tried it on a bright afternoon, and while I spent more time wobbling than gliding, it was a great way to pass the time.

If you prefer to stay dry, you can always join a boat excursion. Several firms provide small boat rides down the river, providing a relaxing opportunity to see the sights without breaking a sweat. It's a laid-back way to appreciate the Onyar, especially if you're traveling with family or simply want to unwind and let someone else handle the navigating.

In many ways, the River Onyari is the throbbing heart of Girona. Whether you're meandering along its banks, passing one of its famed bridges, or simply resting by the water with a cup of coffee, the river exudes peace and beauty throughout the city. It's a site where history and current life coexist, where colorful houses reflect on the lake, and where each turn provides a fresh perspective.

So, take your time with Onyar. Explore its bridges, shoot its magnificence, and even take a paddle in its waters. Just be warned: after you've spent time by the river, you'll find yourself returning to it over and over. Something about its peaceful appeal draws you in, and before you realize it, the River Onyar has become the setting for some of your most memorable moments in Girona.

Chapter 18

OFF THE BEATEN PATH GIRONA

Girona may be famous for its iconic cathedral, the scenic River Onyar, and the ancient elegance of its Old Town, but what if I told you there's so much more to this Catalan city than the usual tourist attractions? After spending time roaming Girona's small alleyways and exploring its lesser-known corners, I discovered a side of the city that many visitors never see. These are the sites that don't appear on every vacation itinerary—the hidden treasures, secret streets, and distinct districts that give Girona its genuine personality. And believe me, if you take the time to go beyond the well-trodden roads, Girona will surprise you more than you ever anticipated.

Allow me to take you on a journey through off-the-beaten-path Girona, where the crowds thin out and you can see the city as a native. Believe me, these hidden jewels are worth hunting out. Whether you're a first-time visitor trying to go deeper or a seasoned Girona enthusiast looking for new adventures, these spots will show you the city in a completely new light.

Hidden Gems: Lesser-Known Attractions

Girona's prominent attractions—its cathedral, Passeig de la Muralla, and Jewish Quarter—are unquestionably spectacular, but it's often the smaller, lesser-known sites that leave the most lasting impression. There's something special about finding an unexpected jewel while roaming through a city, and Girona offers plenty of them.

Jardins de la Francesa is one such hidden gem, located near the Monastery of Sant Pere de Galligants. This peaceful little retreat is ideal for getting away from the crowds and spending some quiet time. The gardens, with their stone walks, fragrant flowers, and benches with panoramic views of the city, feel like a secret sanctuary. I discovered this site by mistake one day while touring the Sant Pereneighborhood, and it quickly became one of my favorite spots to relax. The gardens are small, but that's part of their appeal—you'll frequently find yourself alone here, with only the sound of birdsong and the odd flutter of the wind through the trees.

Casa Masó, located on Carrer Ballesteries, is another lesser-known hidden gem. This stunning modernist home, which previously belonged to architect Rafael Masó, is a must-see for admirers of early twentieth-century design. Unlike the enormous facades of Barcelona's most iconic modernist structures, Casa Masó is softly elegant and blends in with its surroundings. Inside, you'll find original furniture, art, and decorative features in the Catalan modernist style, all in their pristine condition. The mansion also has stunning views of the Onyar River, making it an ideal location for both history historians and design enthusiasts.

My favorite hidden gem in Girona is the Arab Baths (Banys Àrabs). These 12th-century baths, located near Girona Cathedral, provide an intriguing peek into the city's medieval past. While the baths are no longer active, the design is beautiful, combining Romanesque and Islamic influences. The frigidarium (cold room) is especially lovely, with its octagonal pool and columns that reach up to a domed ceiling. This spot was wonderfully tranquil for me—a quiet escape from the hustle and bustle of the Old Town. It's simple to visualize the room as it once was, complete with splashing water and quiet discussion.

Secret Streets in the Old Town

Girona's Old Town is full of winding passageways and hidden corners, and while the major streets are crowded with tourists, there are plenty of secret streets just waiting to be explored. These lesser-known pathways can lead to unexpected sights, offbeat stores, and moments of pure wonder.

One of my favorite secret streets is Carrer de la Força, which runs parallel to the more well-known Carrer dels Alemanys. While Carrer dels Alemanys is packed with businesses and tourists, Carrer de la Força feels like a step back in time. The roadway is small and cobblestoned, with ancient stone structures towering above. It's very uncommon to find yourself alone here, especially in the early morning or late afternoon, because the silence allows you to truly appreciate the details—the wrought-iron balconies, the ancient entrances, the ivy climbing up the walls. Walking along Carrer de la Força seems like you've discovered a hidden aspect of the Old Town that most visitors never get to explore.

Carrer de les Mosques is another hidden gem in the Old Town, a small street off Carrer de la Força. Blink and you could miss it, but believe me, it's worth looking for. This street is so tiny that you can almost touch both walls at once, and it's lined with cute, ivy-covered buildings. There's a genuine sense of closeness here, as if you've stumbled across a secret nook of Girona that most people miss. As you travel down Carrer de les Mosques, you'll feel as if you're privy to a secret that only a few lucky people ever learn.

Explore Carrer dels Cúndaro, a hidden gem near the Jewish Quarter. This narrow, stone-paved lane leads through one of the most evocative portions of the Old Town, past hidden courtyards, historic arches, and small artisan shops. I like walking along this street at nightfall, when the mellow glow of the streetlamps made long shadows on the walls and the sounds of the city seemed to disappear.

Explore Girona's Lesser-Known Neighborhoods

While the Old Town is the beating heart of Girona, the city is much more than just its medieval core. Explore Girona's lesser-known areas, which are full of charm, character, and local culture.

One of my favorite spots to visit is Sant Narcís, a district just outside the Old Town with tree-lined streets, little parks, and local cafés. While not as historically significant as the Jewish Quarter or Barri Vell, Sant Narcís provides a welcome counterpoint to the rush and bustle of the city center. Locals are seen here going about their regular activities, such as shopping at the neighborhood market, having coffee at sidewalk cafés, and chatting with their neighbors. It's an excellent area to explore Girona's more residential side, and it also has some fantastic eateries that aren't on the tourist radar.

Montjuïc is a hidden gem of a neighborhood, located on a hill overlooking the city. The journey to Montjuïccan is hard, but the views from the summit are well worth it. From here, you can see the entire city stretch out under you, with the Girona Cathedral rising majestically in the background. Montjuïcit is a peaceful residential region with tiny streets and lovely cottages that appear to cling to the hillside. It's ideal for a leisurely afternoon stroll, and if you're searching for a quiet getaway from the crowds, this is the place to go.

For something altogether different, visit La Devesa, Girona's green lung. Parc de la Devesa, a huge park with tall plane trees, spacious pathways, and plenty of room to rest, is the focal point of this area. I enjoyed going here in the early evening, when folks congregated for picnics, jogs, and leisurely strolls across the park. It's an excellent place to recharge your batteries after a day of sightseeing, and it also has a fantastic weekly market where you can buy fresh fruit, local cheeses, and a variety of Catalan delights.

Unique Museums and Galleries

Girona is home to some well-known museums, including the Museum of Jewish History and the Girona Art Museum, but the city also boasts several lesser-known museums and galleries that are well worth seeing, especially if you're seeking for something unique.

One of the most unusual museums I discovered is the Museu del Cinema (Museum of Cinema), which is located on Carrer de la Sèquia. This eccentric small museum is a must-see for film fans and anybody interested in cinema history. The museum has a remarkable collection of early film technology, ranging from magic lanterns to old cameras, and it provides an interesting insight at how moving pictures evolved over time. What I liked best about this museum is how interactive it is—there are lots of hands-on exhibits where you can try your hand at making your own cartoons or understand how early filmmakers did their special effects. It's the type of spot where you may lose track of time, and I ended up spending far more time here than I had intended.

Another hidden gem is Galeria d'Art Dolors Ventós, a modest modern art gallery on Carrer de les Ballesteries. This gallery features the work of local Catalan artists, and the exhibitions vary frequently, so there is always something new to view. I went in one afternoon with no expectations and was pleasantly pleased by the diversity of artwork on exhibit, which ranged from abstract paintings to recycled-material sculptures. The gallery is modest but intimate, and it feels like a place where creativity thrives. If you enjoy modern art, this gallery is a must-see.

Girona's Best Kept Local Secrets

Of course, no chapter on off-the-beaten-path Girona would be complete without mentioning some of the city's best-kept local secrets. These are the places and experiences that you won't find in any guidebooks, the ones that make you feel like you've discovered something truly unique.

One of Girona's best-kept secrets is the Plaça de Sant Feliu, a modest area near the Sant Feliu Basilica. While most people head to the nearby church, this calm little area is largely unknown. It's a peaceful area to sit and drink a coffee, or simply admire the surrounding buildings. What makes this area truly unique is that it is home to one of Girona's strangest legends—the Lioness of Girona. A stone figure of a lioness ascending upward sits atop a little column, and folklore says that kissing the lioness's rear end will assure your safe return to Girona. Yes, you read it right. I observed several courageous folks plant a kiss on the lioness's rear, and while I didn't participate, I can't deny that it makes for a humorous and memorable photo opportunity.

Another local secret is tavern El Vermutet, a little tavern hidden down a side street near Plaça de la Independència. This modest small bar is popular among locals for its excellent vermouth and tapas, and it offers a casual, no-frills atmosphere that I adored. The bar is small—just enough room for a few tables—but the atmosphere is warm and inviting. I spent a quiet afternoon here, sipping vermouth and eating olives, anchovies, and crunchy fried potatoes. If you're searching for an authentic, off-the-beaten-path dining experience, El Vermutet is the place to be.

Finally, if you're looking for some live music, visit Sunset Jazz Club, a hidden gem near the Pont de Pedra. This little bar is the ideal spot to unwind after a day of exploring, and the live jazz performances are exceptional. The gloomy lighting, warm setting, and delicious cocktails create the feeling of a secret hideaway, and it's easy to lose track of time. Sunset Jazz Club is one of Girona's best-kept secrets, whether you're a jazz fan or simply seeking for a fun night out.

Exploring off-the-beaten-path Girona is like peeling back the layers of the city to reveal its hidden jewels. From hidden streets to lesser-known museums, eccentric legends to quiet local bars, Girona has so much more to offer than meets the eye. So, the next time you're in the city, take some time to stroll off the major roads, follow your curiosity, and see where it takes you. You might just find your own favorite hidden gem.

Chapter 19

SUSTAINABLE AND ENVIRONMENTALLY FRIENDLY TRAVEL IN GIRONA

As travelers, we often fantasize about new destinations, new experiences, and taking in the beauty of faraway places—but there's an added layer to consider: how to do all of that without leaving a path of environmental harm. Girona, with its gorgeous streets, breathtaking surroundings, and dynamic local culture, is a great destination for anyone looking to travel responsibly and sustainably. It's a city that has embraced eco-friendly methods while maintaining its charm, and after spending time here, I understood how simple—and rewarding—it can be to make greener choices while still enjoying everything this Catalan treasure has to offer.

Now, I'm not going to propose you start cycling to Girona from wherever you are (unless you enjoy extreme sports). But with a few changes to your travel routine—such as choosing an eco-friendly hotel, supporting local businesses, or simply being more conscious of your carbon footprint—you can enjoy the best of Girona while also helping to maintain this beautiful corner of the world. Let's look at some simple methods to make your trip to Girona more sustainable without compromising any of the enjoyment.

Environmentally Friendly Hotels and Accommodations

Choosing an eco-friendly place to stay is an important first step toward sustainable travel. Girona is home to various hotels and accommodations that stress comfort and style while also making a concerted effort to lessen their environmental effect. Whether you're looking for a luxurious hotel or a cozy guesthouse, there are lots of options that will allow you to sleep peacefully while also helping the environment.

Hotel Nord 1901, located in the heart of Girona, just a few steps from the Onyar River, stands out as an environmentally aware option. This boutique hotel has embraced sustainability in a variety of ways, including utilizing energy-efficient lighting and water-saving fixtures and offering organic, locally produced food in their restaurant. What I like best about Hotel Nord 1901—aside from the rooftop pool with a view of the cathedral, which everyone enjoys—is its devotion to waste reduction. The rooms are free of those awful single-use plastic toiletries (you know the ones), and instead provide refillable, eco-friendly goods. It's ideal for tourists looking for a touch of luxury without feeling guilty about their environmental impact.

Mas La Casassa, a typical Catalan farmhouse turned eco-friendly guesthouse located just a short drive from Girona, offers something a little more rustic but equally attractive. Surrounded by nature, this rustic resort feels like a hidden sanctuary, but what truly distinguishes it is its commitment to sustainability. The owners have installed solar panels to power much of the property, and they prioritize recycling and composting. The rooms are very charming, with wooden beams and stone walls that make you feel like you've gone back in time while still enjoying modern amenities. Waking up to the sound of birds chirping and the scent of fresh mountain air is one of those simple pleasures that makes you love nature even more.

If you wish to stay closer to the Costa Brava while still visiting Girona, Hotel Terramarin Llafranc is a great eco-friendly choice. The hotel is part of the Costa Brava Sustainable Tourism initiative, which aims to reduce water and energy usage while also supporting local artists and organic farmers. After a day of visiting Girona, you can relax by the coast, knowing that your stay benefits both the environment and the local people.

Sustainable Restaurants and Cafes

Food is one of the most enjoyable aspects of travel, and Girona has plenty of exquisite Catalan cuisine to offer. However, eating responsibly does not imply compromising flavor; in fact, some of the greatest meals I had in Girona were at restaurants and cafés that emphasized local, organic, and seasonal food. Supporting these businesses not only allows you to eat healthier, but it also helps to cut food miles and support local farmers and producers.

BionBo, a modern, eco-conscious restaurant on Carrer de la Creu, 10, is one of my absolute faves. Joan Carles Sánchez, the chef, is passionate about using locally produced, organic ingredients to create recipes that are both delicious and environmentally responsible. The menu changes seasonally to match what's fresh and available, and the dishes are full of flavor. I had the pleasure of dining here on a beautiful evening, beginning with a plate of roasted veggies from a nearby farm and ending with a scrumptious, ethically produced fish. The presentation was exquisite, and you could taste the attention that went into each bite.

For something more casual, Fika Girona is a lovely café near Plaça de la Independència. They specialize in healthful, plant-based meals, and their coffee comes from ethical, fair-trade producers. It's the kind of restaurant where you can get a smoothie bowl or avocado toast in the morning and feel good about it since it's all produced with sustainable ingredients. In addition, they prioritize waste reduction by using biodegradable packaging and offering discounts if you bring your own reusable cup.

If you're looking for something sweet, La Bombonera serves a unique take on traditional Catalan pastries, all created with organic, locally sourced ingredients. Their xuixo, a sweet, fried pastry filled with custard, is delicious—and the fact that it's produced with responsibly sourced ingredients makes it even more fulfilling.

How to Travel Green in Girona

Girona's tiny size and well-connected public transportation system make green travel surprisingly easy. One of the simplest methods to limit your environmental effect while traveling is to walk or cycle as much as possible, and Girona makes this not only practical but also pleasurable.

Girona is a walkers' paradise. The Old Town's tiny streets and scenic squares are best explored on foot, and walking often lets you to uncover hidden corners that you would have missed if you were driving. Furthermore, walking helps you burn off the excess calories from the patatas bravas and crema catalana. Win-win, right?

If you're feeling more daring (or if you've had too many xuixos), Girona is an excellent cycling destination. There are multiple bike rental shops throughout the city, and Girona's position as a cycling hotspot means that there are numerous well-marked bike trails to explore. For a picturesque ride, I recommend the Ruta del Carrilet, an old railway route turned into a cycling path that connects Girona to the seaside. The route takes you through beautiful countryside and charming communities, making it an excellent way to explore the region's beauty while leaving a low carbon imprint.

When you need to travel further afield, Girona's public transit is both efficient and environmentally sustainable. The city's bus system is simple to use, and daily trains connect Girona to Barcelona, the Costa Brava, and elsewhere. The AVE high-speed rail is a great choice for longer travels because it is fast, pleasant, and far more environmentally friendly than flying or driving. I rode the AVE to Barcelona, and the ride was not only short (approximately 40 minutes), but also quite smooth—far superior to dealing with airport security, in my opinion.

Supporting Local Businesses and Communities

One of the most effective methods to travel sustainably is to patronize local businesses and contribute to the local economy. In Girona, this entails shopping at markets, purchasing from craftsmen, and favoring family-owned enterprises over giant chains. By doing so, you help to preserve the city's unique character while ensuring that your money goes directly to the people who live and work there.

Visits to Girona's busy food market, Mercat del Lleó, were one of my favorite ways to support the local community. The market, located on Plaça Calvet i Rubalcaba, is a sensory delight, with stalls brimming with fresh fruit, local cheeses, cured meats, and more. I enjoyed going through the market, talking with the vendors, and gathering supplies for a picnic by the river. Not only is the food here extremely fresh, but it also helps to support local farmers and producers.

Carrer Ballesteries offers a genuinely unique shopping experience, with a mix of artisan stores and boutiques selling anything from handcrafted ceramics to locally manufactured fabrics. One of my favorite finds was La Volta, an artist organization that displays the work of local artisans. Everything from jewelry to home decor is available here, all created by artists residing in Girona. I bought a beautiful hand-painted ceramic dish as a keepsake, and it felt nice to know that my money was going to a local artist rather than a mass-produced factory item.

Reduce Your Carbon Footprint While Traveling

Reducing your carbon impact when traveling does not have to be difficult. In truth, even, easy changes can have a tremendous impact, especially when visiting a walkable and environmentally conscious city like Girona.

One simple approach to reduce your carbon footprint is to fly less—which is totally possible when visiting Girona. If you are traveling from elsewhere in Europe, consider taking the train instead of flying. Girona is well-connected by rail, and the high-speed train network makes it easy to get there from major cities such as Barcelona, Madrid, and even Paris. Not only is taking the train significantly more environmentally responsible than flying, but it's also a lot more comfortable mode of transportation—no long security lines, no luggage fees, and plenty of legroom.

Avoiding single-use plastics while visiting Girona is another method to lessen your carbon footprint. Bring a reusable water bottle—Girona has plenty of public fountains for refilling, and the tap water is entirely safe to drink. Many cafés and restaurants in Girona will gladly refill your bottle for you, especially if you order something else.

Finally, think about slow travel—spending more time in one location rather than jumping from city to city. Staying in Girona for a prolonged amount of time not only minimizes your carbon footprint from traveling, but also allows you to get more connected to the city and its culture. I discovered that taking my time exploring Girona, rather than hurrying through a packed itinerary, resulted in a much more meaningful and delightful experience.

Responsible Wildlife Watching and Tours

While Girona isn't particularly known for its wildlife, the surrounding Costa Brava region provides numerous possibilities for animal viewing, from birding in the wetlands to spotting dolphins along the coast. However, it is critical to engage in these activities appropriately so that your presence does not hurt the animals or their environments.

If you enjoy birdwatching, I highly recommend visiting the Aiguamolls de l'Empordà, a beautiful wetland region just a short drive from Girona. The park is home to a diverse range of bird species, including flamingos, herons, and storks, and is a paradise for wildlife enthusiasts. The key to proper wildlife watching is to observe from a distance, avoid disturbing the animals, and always stick to approved trails to safeguard their ecosystems. I spent a tranquil morning here, watching the birds soar effortlessly across the river, and it served as a magical reminder of the importance of preserving these natural spaces.

For visitors looking to explore the Mediterranean coast, various eco-friendly boat cruises operate along the Costa Brava, with opportunities to see dolphins, seagulls, and sea turtles. These tours are offered by firms that stress sustainability, utilizing low-impact boats and following stringent criteria to guarantee that wildlife is not disturbed. I took a small group trip one afternoon and was ecstatic when we saw a pod of dolphins playing in the waters. It was a fantastic experience, made even better by the fact that our tour was performed in an environmentally friendly manner.

Traveling sustainably in Girona is not only doable, but extremely rewarding. From staying in eco-friendly hotels to supporting local businesses, dining sustainably, and lowering your carbon footprint, there are numerous ways to enjoy this lovely city while making a difference. Whether you're meandering along the River Onyar, cycling through the countryside, or indulging in a great dinner produced with local products, Girona's sustainable travel philosophy is all about enjoying the simple pleasures while remaining mindful of the world around you. So go ahead and embrace green travel; Girona will show you how lovely and enjoyable sustainable tourism can be.

Chapter 20

GIRONA'S LOCAL MARKETS

One of my favorite methods to get to know a new city is by exploring its markets. The rush and bustle, the brilliant colors, the numerous stalls of fresh produce, local delicacies, and handmade crafts all contribute to a true sense of place—literally and figuratively. In Girona, the markets are where the magic occurs. They are vivacious, full of character, and brimming with Catalan flavors. During my visits, I made it a point to explore Girona's markets, and I immediately discovered that they are more than just places to shop; they are a reflection of the city's personality.

Girona's markets provide an opportunity to immerse oneself in local life. You'll find grandmothers chatting with sellers, chefs selecting the freshest items for the evening's dinner service, and travelers like me admiring the cheese, jamón, and olives on exhibit. Girona's markets have something for everyone, whether you're a foodie, a curious visitor, or just looking for a good deal. So join us for a leisurely stroll through the best local markets, complete with laughter and food tasting.

Mercat del Lleó: Girona's Main Market

If you ask a local where to find the freshest produce in Girona, they will direct you to Mercat del Lleó. This indoor market, located on Plaça Calvet i Rubalcaba, is the beating heart of Girona's food culture. It's where locals go to get anything from eggs in the morning to seafood for dinner, and let me tell you, it's a sensory explosion in the nicest way.

When I first went into Mercat del Lleó, I felt as if I had wandered into a foodie's dream. The smell of freshly baked bread, the sight of gleaming eggplants and luscious tomatoes stacked high, the sound of vendors shouting prices in rapid-fire Catalan—it's the kind of place where you might easily lose yourself for the entire morning. The market is divided into sections, each dedicated to a distinct sort of food, so whether you're looking for fruit, meat, seafood, or cheese, there's a place for you.

I began my tour in the fish area, where the counters were stacked high with everything from glistening sardines to gigantic prawns that appeared to have jumped straight out of the Mediterranean. The fishmongers were hard at work, deftly filleting fish and cracking open oysters, while locals waited up to get the freshest catch for their supper. It's a remarkable demonstration of Girona's proximity to the sea, and if you're intending to cook while you're here, here is the place to get your ingredients.

Next, I went to the cheese section, which was, unsurprisingly, my personal version of heaven. Stall after stall was loaded with rounds of manchego, wedges of garrotxa (a creamy and slightly sour Catalan goat's cheese), and a variety of other cheesy treats. I couldn't resist trying a few other types—one of the vendors was more than pleased to give me a tasting tour of their selection, and I left with a wedge of Tupi, a strong, fermented cheese that's not for the faint of heart but incredibly great if you like intense flavors.

However, Mercat del Lleó is more than simply raw materials; it's also a terrific spot to eat. Several kiosks serve cooked foods, and I ended up at one that specializes in botifarra, a classic Catalan sausage. Grilled fresh, served with toast and roasted peppers, it was the ideal snack to keep me going while I toured the remainder of the market. Of course, I washed it down with a tiny glass of vermut—when in Girona, right?

Street Markets and Seasonal Events

While Mercat del Lleóis is Girona's primary market, the city also hosts a number of street markets and seasonal events throughout the year. These are more than just shopping destinations; they are bustling social gatherings where locals and visitors can socialize, enjoy the atmosphere, and, of course, buy for unique items.

The Fira de Sant Narcís, held during the Festa de Sant Narcís in October, was a memorable street fair for me. This is Girona's largest festival, and the streets are bustling with kiosks selling everything from handcrafted crafts to local specialties. The market winds through the streets of the Old Town, and I spent hours strolling from vendor to stall, admiring the quality of the pottery, jewelry, and textiles on show. There were also lots of food vendors selling local goodies like panellets (small almond cakes) and castanyes (roasted chestnuts), which were the ideal snack to keep me warm as the autumn chill set in.

Another fantastic street market is the Fira de Nadal (Christmas Market), which takes place throughout December. If you're lucky enough to visit Girona during the holiday season, you must see this market. It's hosted in Plaça de la Independència and has festive kiosks selling Christmas decorations, homemade presents, and seasonal delicacies. There's something special about sipping hot chocolate while wandering the market's dazzling lights—plus, it's the ideal spot to pick up some particularly Catalan Christmas ornaments, such as the caganer (a mischievous little figure found in Catalan nativity scenes).

Best Places to Buy Local Produce

Girona has several of choices for purchasing local goods outside of the Mercat del Lleó. Whether you're going to cook at your Airbnb or simply want to bring home a taste of Girona, here are some of the best places to get fresh, local produce.

For a more intimate, local feel, I recommend visiting the Mercat de Salt, a smaller, less touristic market just outside of Girona in the nearby town of Salt. This market is where residents go for their weekly shopping, and you'll find a wide variety of fresh fruits and vegetables gathered from nearby farms. It's less crowded than Mercat del Lleó, and the vendors are extremely courteous, frequently offering free samples or a quick conversation about their products. I left this market with a bag full of sun-ripened tomatoes, fresh herbs, and the finest strawberries I'd ever tasted.

The weekly farmers' market, held every Tuesday and Saturday morning at the Plaça de la Independència, is another excellent source of local produce. This open-air market is a true find, with kiosks selling everything from freshly baked bread to organic veggies, local honey, and handmade cheese. The vendors are typically farmers themselves, so you may ask them about where their products come from and how they are farmed. I bought some organic olive oil and a bottle of local wine, which made ideal gifts for friends back home (and perhaps a little treat for myself).

For a more curated assortment, visit Casa Moner, a gourmet boutique on Carrer del Nord, 4. This shop specializes on high-quality local items, including as cured meats, jams, olive oils, and handmade sweets. It's the kind of store where you might easily spend an hour perusing, and I couldn't leave without buying a jar of melmelada de figues (fig jam) and a packet of torrons (traditional Catalan nougat).

Farmers' Markets Around Girona

If you have the opportunity to go beyond the city, the farmers' markets in Girona are definitely worth the journey. These markets sell the freshest produce, frequently cultivated just a few kilometers from the city, and are an excellent opportunity to experience the region's agricultural bounty.

One of the greatest farmers' markets I attended was in Banyoles, which is about 20 minutes' drive from Girona. Every Wednesday, the Plaça Major has a market with kiosks selling anything from seasonal vegetables to local cheeses, charcuterie, and freshly baked bread. Banyoles is famed for its gorgeous lake, so after buying up some picnic provisions at the market, I spent the afternoon by the water, admiring the scenery and nibbling on local goodies.

Besalú, a medieval village, holds a popular farmers' market every Tuesday in its town center. The market in Besalú is a must-see, adding to the city's medieval charm and gorgeous architecture. I enjoyed meandering around the little alleyways, stopping at market stalls to pick up local honey, fresh herbs, and some of the greatest mató (a Catalan fresh cheese) I'd ever tasted.

Food Tasting and Sampling in Markets

One of the most enjoyable aspects of visiting Girona's markets is that sampling the wares is not only encouraged—but virtually required. I can't tell you how many times I found myself snacking on pieces of fuet (a Catalan cured sausage), cubes of cheese, or portions of freshly baked bread as I moved from stand to stall. It's like a tapas tour without the need to sit down.

Many merchants at Mercat del Lleó are delighted to offer you a taste of their products, whether it's a slice of jamón ibérico or a tablespoon of olive oil. One seller in particular stuck out to me—a cheerful cheesemonger who, upon seeing my wide-eyed enthusiasm for all the cheeses on display, insisted on giving me a crash course on Catalan cheese. I tried everything from the mild, creamy matóto to the aforementioned Tupi, which he described as "for people who like their cheese to punch them in the face" (his words, not mine). It was peppery, funky, and completely fantastic.

The same is true for the farmers' markets outside Girona. In Banyoles, I was handed slices of delicious, sun-ripened peaches by a farmer eager to show off his produce. In Besalú, I sampled a range of local honeys, each having a particular flavor depending on the flowers the bees had foraged from. One was delicate and flowery, while another had a thick, almost caramel-like flavor. Naturally, I purchased both.

If you're a foodie, these markets are the best places to delight your taste senses and try new cuisines. And, let's be honest, there's no better way to decide whether you want to buy that wedge of cheese or bottle of olive oil than to try it first. Furthermore, it's an excellent way to strike up a conversation with the sellers, many of whom are eager to offer stories about their products, farms, and the history of their family companies.

Girona's markets are more than just places to shop; they are bustling hubs of local life, bursting with Catalan flavors, scents, and colors. Whether you're exploring the stalls at Mercat del Lleó, sampling cheese at a farmers' market, or sipping vermutat at a street market, these activities provide a genuine taste of the region's culture. Exploring Girona's markets was one of the pleasures of my trip for me—each one seemed like a mini-adventure, and the gems I discovered (both food and non-edible) were some of my favorite keepsakes.

So, the next time you're in Girona, don't just visit the standard tourist attractions. Go to the markets, talk to the vendors, sample whatever you can, and immerse yourself in the delightful, colorful world of Girona local life. Just remember to bring an empty bag for all the things you'll want to take home.

Chapter 21

GIRONA FOR RETURNING VISITORS

So you've been to Girona before and now you're returning. Perhaps the colorful cottages along the River Onyar attracted you, or perhaps the twisting lanes of the Barri Vell piqued your interest. Maybe it's the food—who can pass up another round of patatas bravas and crème catalana? Whatever drove you here in the first place, returning to Girona as an experienced visitor adds a whole new depth of discovery. The beauty of this city is that there is always something new to discover, even if you've been along these cobblestone streets before.

On my second (and third, and, let's be honest, fourth) trip to Girona, I fell even more in love with its quieter, less touristic areas. I uncovered hidden gems that I hadn't noticed on my previous visit, reunited with

189

residents I met along the route, and had new experiences that made the city feel new all over again. Girona, with its medieval charm and laid-back feel, is one of those locations that keeps surprising you no matter how many times you go.

So, if you are a returning tourist to Girona, welcome back! Here's how to explore the city you already love, from hidden jewels to new developments, advanced tours to catching up with the residents who make it seem like home.

Rediscovering Girona: New Experiences

Returning to a city can seem similar to visiting an old friend. Walking past familiar monuments, revisiting beloved cafés, and retracing your steps through streets that feel like old friends can be comforting. But just because you've been here before doesn't mean you won't find something new around every turn.

On my second trip to Girona, I made it a point to explore areas of the city that I hadn't had chance to see on my first visit. Sure, the Girona Cathedral and the Passeig de la Muralla are must-sees, but this city has so much more to offer than just those sights. This time, I went to the Sant Daniel Valley, a tranquil, green sanctuary located just a short walk from the city center. Many first-time tourists overlook it, but it's well worth the trip for its stunning scenery and the calm Sant Daniel Monastery, where you can immerse yourself in the history and serenity of this centuries-old sanctuary.

Another unique experience I tried during a return visit was a hot air balloon flight over Girona and the surrounding countryside. Let me tell you, viewing Girona from the air is a completely different ballgame. The view of the Pyrenees in the background, the rolling hills, and the ancient rooftops of the city below make you feel as if you're hovering above a picture. If you're looking for something that will genuinely blow your mind on your second (or third) trip, I highly recommend it.

There are also many new activities that emerge during the year. For example, if you visit during the annual Temps de Florsflower festival in May, you'll be able to see the city turned into a flowery heaven. Throughout the week-long event, the Old Town is adorned with exquisite floral displays, sculptures, and gardens, transforming recognizable streets into pieces of beauty. Even if you've been to Girona before, seeing it in bloom is like discovering it for the first time.

Updates and Recent Developments in the City

Cities are always evolving, and Girona is no exception. While the medieval walls and centuries-old cathedrals remain unchanged, there have been numerous new projects in the city that make it feel new, even to regular visitors.

The Culinary Spaceat El Celler de Can Roca, one of Girona's most exciting recent additions, formally opened to the public after years of being the realm of the legendary Roca brothers. While getting a reservation at El Celler de Can Roca (consistently ranked as one of the best restaurants in the world) remains difficult, the new Culinary Space offers cooking workshops, wine tastings, and special events for those of us who may be unable to secure a table at the restaurant. During my last visit, I enrolled in one of their cooking classes, where I learnt how to create suquet de peix, a classic Catalan fish stew, from scratch. Let's just say my cooking abilities have never been the same (in a nice manner, of course).

Another new development in Girona is the redevelopment of the Plaça de Catalunya area. This major center has always been a thriving hub, but recent renovations have given it a new face, with more green spaces, public art, and pedestrian-friendly sections. It's a terrific place to sit with a coffee and people-watch, and it serves as an excellent starting point for exploring some of the city's lesser-known streets.

In terms of new dining options, Nu Girona, a modern, trendy restaurant, has been a favorite among both locals and visitors. The restaurant combines traditional Catalan ingredients with modern technology to create a tasting menu that is both unique and delicious. I tried their calçots with romesco sauce, a seasonal Catalan delicacy traditionally grilled over an open flame, and it was a delight. If you are a foodie, Nu Girona is a must-see on your return trip.

Hidden Gems for Experienced Travellers

Even if you think you've seen everything, Girona still has plenty of hidden jewels to find. These are the types of sites you won't find in guidebooks, but which make the city feel even more special the second time around.

One such hidden gem is the Jardins dels Alemanys, a peaceful, green park in the heart of the Old Town. I discovered this nook while visiting the city's historic walls, and it immediately became one of my favorite places to get away from the crowds. The gardens are tiny but well-designed, with chairs placed around to sit and enjoy the view of the city below. It's an ideal location for a mid-afternoon break, especially if you've been walking all day.

The Museu d'Història de Girona, located in a former monastery, is an often-overlooked hidden gem. While not as spectacular as some of the city's other museums, it provides an intriguing glimpse at Girona's history, from Roman times to the present. The exhibitions are well-curated, and there is a lovely courtyard where you can sit and think on the history you've just learned.

For those who enjoy a nice trek, a lesser-known road leads from Girona to the adjacent Castle of Sant Miquel, a ruined castle with panoramic views of the city and surrounding countryside. The hike is difficult, but the reward at the summit is worth every step. Plus, because it's off the beaten road, you'll probably have the place to yourself—just you, the wind, and the breathtaking vista.

Advanced Tours and Specialized Itineraries

If you've already visited the main attractions, it's time to explore advanced tours and specialist itineraries that delve deeper into Girona's culture, history, and landscapes. These trips are designed for experienced tourists like you who want to see Girona from a different perspective.

A Jewish heritage tour of Girona was one of the most fascinating tours I took during my return visit. While I had roamed through the Jewish Quarter on my previous visit, this guided tour provided a much better grasp of the area's history. We visited the Museum of Jewish History, explored the old mikveh (ritual bath), and learned about Girona's Jewish community, which thrived before being evicted during the Spanish Inquisition. It was a strong, emotive encounter that deepened my perspective of the city.

Explore Salvador Dalí's life and work in Girona with this wonderful itinerary for art enthusiasts. The tour begins in Girona, where you will visit Dalí-related monuments, then continues to Figueres, home to the bizarre Dalí Theatre-Museum. This is the perfect method to immerse yourself in Dalí's unique and innovative world. Furthermore, Figueres is only a short train journey from Girona, making it a convenient day trip.

For something more adventurous, there are specialized cycling excursions that capitalize on Girona's position as a cycling hotspot. These tours range from easy rides through the countryside to challenging multi-day cycling expeditions in the Pyrenees. On one of my travels, I took a guided bike tour along the Ruta del Carrilet, an old railway line turned cycling path that connects Girona to the Costa Brava. It was the ideal balance of scenic beauty, history, and physical exertion, and at the end of the day, I felt like I'd seen a side of Girona that most visitors never see.

Reconnecting with the Girona Locals

One of the best parts of returning to Girona is the opportunity to reconnect with the people. During my first trip, I encountered a few kind people—shop owners, café baristas, and the occasional tour guide. On my subsequent visits, I made it a point to seek them out again, and it felt like we had picked up right where we left off. Girona's residents are friendly and hospitable, and they make you feel like you're a part of the town even if you're only visiting.

If you're staying at the same hotel or guesthouse as before, don't be timid about greeting the personnel. Chances are they will remember you, especially if you had a good chat the first time. On my second trip, I stayed at Hotel Nord 1901, where the receptionist greeted me like an old friend, inquiring about my previous trip and recommending new restaurants. It's the small connections that make returning to Girona so memorable.

One of the finest ways to reconnect with locals is to return to the cafés and restaurants you enjoyed previously. On each visit, I made a point of stopping at La Fabrica, a quiet café popular with both locals and foreigners. After a couple of trips, the barista remembered me, and by the third time I returned, we were chatting like old friends about the greatest cycling routes in Girona (he is also a rider). These tiny connections make Girona feel like a second home rather than a tourist destination.

Looking to connect with Girona's creative community? Visit La Volta, an artist collective and cultural center in the Sant Narcís area. They provide regular events, exhibitions, and seminars, and it's an excellent place to meet local artists, designers, and musicians. On my last trip, I attended a pottery workshop and spent the afternoon conversing with the artist who led the class. She provided me wonderful recommendations for more hidden jewels in the city that only locals know about.

Returning to Girona is like seeing an old friend—you know and love the city, yet there is always something new to discover. Whether you're discovering hidden gardens, taking expert excursions, or simply bonding with the people, Girona reveals itself in layers. Every return provides new experiences, memories, and deeper connections to this lovely Catalan city.

So, if you've already been to Girona and are wondering if there's more to see, the answer is a resounding yes. There are always fresh nooks to discover, hidden gems to find, and familiar faces to greet you again. And who knows. Maybe by the third or fourth visit, you'll feel like a resident. Don't forget to swing by your favorite café for a cafè amb llet—they should remember your order by now.

Chapter 22

UNIQUE ITINERARIES & SAMPLE PLANS

If you're anything like me, half the fun comes from organizing a trip. Maybe not half, but it's a critical component of getting the most out of your trip experience. Girona is a city that welcomes all types of visitors—whether you're here for the history, the gastronomy, the adventure, or simply to soak up the vibe, there's an itinerary to suit your tastes. I've spent enough time in Girona to understand its rhythm, and I've created a few itineraries to help you see this lovely city in a way that feels new every time you visit.

These itineraries range from a quick, intense journey for first-timers to a week-long adventure for those who wish to delve deeper. I've also created some unique plans, such as gastronomy excursions, cycling adventures, and even a Game of Thrones-themed route for lovers of the program. So pack your bags, bring your spirit of adventure, and let's explore the various ways to discover Girona.

A Three-Day Itinerary for First-Time Visitors

Let's begin with a typical three-day itinerary—the ideal amount of time to sample Girona's top offers without feeling rushed. You'll see the highlights while still having enough time to relax, meander, and discover the unexpected moments that make travel so magical.

Day One: Getting to Know Girona Begin your journey in the Girona Cathedral. Arrive early to avoid crowds and take your time exploring this historic site. Climb the renowned steps, admire the Gothic architecture, and don't miss the Tapestry of Creation inside.

- Next, visit the Jewish Quarter (El Call). Wander around the small, labyrinthine streets, absorb the history, and visit the Museum of Jewish History to have a better knowledge of the city's Jewish past.

- Stop for lunch at Placa de la Independència, which is flanked with outdoor cafés ideal for people-watching. Order a platter of patatas bravas and a café amb llet, then unwind and enjoy the lively atmosphere.

- Spend the afternoon exploring Girona's historic city walls, the Passeig de la Muralla. The panoramic views of the city and surrounding countryside are spectacular, and you'll discover some excellent photo opportunities along the way.

- Finish the day with dinner at BionBo, a local favorite serving wonderful, seasonal meals. Believe me when I say that the tasting menu is worth every meal.

Day 2 covers Art, History, and Culture. Begin your day with a visit to the Girona Art Museum. It is housed in the historic Episcopal Palace and has a collection ranging from Romanesque to contemporary art. Don't speed through—some of the displays are quite engaging, particularly the Romanesque frescoes.

- After your museum excursion, stop into La Fabrica for a full breakfast of avocado toast and freshly made coffee. It is a popular destination for both locals and tourists, particularly those who enjoy riding. Spend the afternoon wandering through La Rambla de la Libertat and its surrounding streets. This is Girona's shopping and café district, ideal for leisurely stroll, browsing stores, and buying up souvenirs.

- For dinner, head to Nu Girona, a modern restaurant that combines traditional Catalan ingredients with modern cooking methods. If calçots are in season, try them with romesco sauce.

Day 3: Day Trip to Costa Brava - Spend your final day exploring Costa Brava. Rent a car or take the bus to the adjacent seaside villages of Cadaqués or Begur. Spend the day lounging on the beach, seeing the picturesque seaside villages, or hiking along the coast. Explore the Dalí Theatre-Museum in Figuereson before returning to Girona. This strange, mind-bending event will keep you chatting about Dalí's peculiarities for days.

A Week in Girona: Exploring beyond the Surface

If you have more time, spending a week in Girona will allow you to fully immerse yourself in the city's culture, history, and surrounds. This tour goes beyond the conventional landmarks and provides a closer look at Girona's hidden gems.

Day One: Arrival and Orientation

- Arrive in Girona and spend the first day getting settled. Take a leisurely walk along the Onyar River, cross the Pont de les Peixateries Velles (the Eiffel Bridge), and become acquainted with the layout of the Old Town.

- If you've been able to secure a reservation at El Celler de Can Roca, enjoy a casual meal. If not, do not worry. Girona has many good dining alternatives, like Llevataps, which offers a modern take on Catalan cuisine.

Day 2: History and Architecture - Visit Girona's Romanesque and Gothic attractions, including Girona Cathedral and Sant Feliu Basilica. In the afternoon, take a guided tour of the Sant Pere de Galligants Monastery, then visit the Arab Baths. These lesser-known locations provide a calm, meditative experience with Girona's medieval heritage.

Day 3: Art and Culture - Set aside a full day for art. Begin with the Museu d'Art de Girona, then walk over to Casa Masó, a stunning specimen of Catalan modernism. The house provides guided tours to experience the lifestyle of Girona's middle class in the early 1900s. For dinner, visit Vadevins, a wine bar specializing in local wines and tapas. It's the ideal way to unwind after a long day of culture.

On day 4, take a day trip to the Pyrenees to get away from the metropolis. You can either join a guided hiking tour or rent a car and explore on your own. The environment is stunning, with snow-capped mountains, crystal-clear lakes, and numerous paths for all fitness levels. For a traditional Catalan meal, visit a tiny village like Besalú or pack a picnic lunch to enjoy outside.

Day 5: Market Day and Cooking Class - Spend the morning at Mercat del Lleó. Learn how to make traditional Catalan dishes such as escalivada, suquet de peix, and crème catalana by purchasing fresh, local ingredients and attending a cooking lesson. In the evening, reward yourself for your efforts by eating the dinner you made. Most cooking classes in Girona include community meals, which is a great chance to meet other visitors and share tales.

Day 6: bicycle and Relaxation - Girona is ideal for bicycle aficionados, so spend the day exploring the countryside on two wheels. Rent a bike and explore Girona's riding trails, such as the Ruta del Carrilet, which connects Girona to the Costa Brava. After a day of cycling, pamper yourself with a spa treatment at Aqva Gerunda Banys Romans. Relax in the warm baths and allow your muscles to unwind after all that exertion.

Day 7: Explore Montjuïc and depart.

- On your last day, take a leisurely trek up to Montjuïc Castle for spectacular views of Girona and surrounding countryside. The difficult hike is worth it for the breathtaking vistas. Afterward, eat a final supper at Rocambolesc, the famed ice cream shop run by the Roca brothers, and take one last wander through Girona before returning home.

Girona and Costa Brava: A Combined Trip Plan

For those who prefer to spend time in both the city and the coast, this combination itinerary offers the best of both worlds: spend half your time in Girona and the other half in the Costa Brava, where you can enjoy sun, sand, and sea.

Days 1-3: Girona Highlights - Follow the 3-day plan for first-time visitors to explore top attractions such as Girona Cathedral, Passeig de la Muralla, and the Jewish Quarter.

Days 4–7: Costa Brava Travel to the seashore and establish yourself in Tossa de Maror Llafranc. Spend your days relaxing at the beach, hiking coastal paths, and visiting attractive seaside communities. Visit Cadaqués, a lovely maritime community where Salvador Dalí once lived. Visit the Dalí House-Museum and explore the town's small, whitewashed streets.

- For a thrill, try sea kayaking along the Costa Brava's rough coastline. You'll paddle past hidden coves, tunnels, and crystal-clear water.

A Four-Day Foodie Tour of Girona

This four-day gourmet trip is intended for individuals who travel with their stomachs. Girona is a city rich with taste, and this itinerary will take you through the best of its culinary scene.

Day 1: Traditional Catalan Cuisine - Visit Mercat del Lleó for fresh fruit, cheese, meat, and shellfish. Grab some nibbles for later and have a modest lunch at one of the market's tapas kiosks.

- Make a dinner reservation at Ca l'Enric, a Michelin-starred restaurant that serves innovative twists on classic Catalan food. Try duck with figs or red prawn carpaccio.

Day 2: Tapas and Wine - Explore the Old Town with a tapas tour, including stops at Zanpanzar for legendary pintxos and La Vedette for crepes and tapas. In the afternoon, attend a wine tasting at Mas Oller, a local winery just outside of Girona. You'll try some of the region's top wines, along with local cheeses and charcuterie.

Day 3 - Michelin Stars and Sweet Treats Begin the day at Rocambolesc, Jordi Roca's ice cream business, for a memorable dessert experience. Warm brioche with ice cream is a popular choice among customers. In the evening, enjoy a multi-course supper at El Celler de Can Roca. It's an unforgettable event, and the cuisine is both art and nourishment.

Day 4: Market Cooking session - Conclude your culinary tour with a hands-on cooking session. In the morning, visit the market to buy goods before heading to a local restaurant to learn how to prepare famous Catalan dishes from a local chef.

A Cycling Tour Itinerary for Girona

Girona has become a cycling paradise, so it only makes sense to build a cycling-specific itinerary for anyone looking to explore the region on two wheels.

Day 1: Getting Acclimated - Rent a bike and go for a brief ride around Old Town. Explore the Jewish Quarter, the Onyar River bridges, and the Girona Cathedral on foot to relax your legs.

Day 2: The Classic Girona Loop - Begin with a ride along the Sant Grau Loop, one of Girona's most popular cycling routes. It's a difficult ride, but it provides breathtaking views of the countryside and the Costa Brava in the distance. End your day with a hearty supper at La Fabrica, a popular bicycle café for both locals and visitors.

On Day 3, take a lengthier cycle to Tossa de Mar along the Ruta del Carriletto. Spend the afternoon lounging on the beach or touring the old fortification that stands above the town.

Day 4: Challenge yourself with the Montseny Mountains. This journey takes you through picturesque forests, past waterfalls, and up some steep slopes. It is not for the faint of heart, but the views from the summit make it all worthwhile.

A Game of Thrones Fan's Two-Day Itinerary

Girona was the filming location for various sequences in King's Landing and Braavos on the popular television series Game of Thrones. This two-day tour will take you to all of the important filming locations.

Day 1: Walking through King's Landing

- Begin your day in the Girona Cathedral, which functioned as the Great Sept of Baelor during Season 6. You will immediately know the majestic staircase where Jaime Lannister encountered the High Sparrow.

- Next, go to the Arab Baths, which served as a filming location for Arya's training in Braavos. The medieval setting feels like something out of Westeros.

- End the day with a Game of Thrones-themed tour of the Jewish Quarter, where many of the Braavos scenes were shot. Your guide will show out important spots and give behind-the-scenes information.

Day 2: Exploring Additional Filming Locations Visit the Monastery of Sant Pere de Galligants, which also serves as the Citadel in Oldtown. The Romanesque structure is stunning and reminiscent of the play. In the afternoon, visit Besalú, a medieval village that served as a backdrop for the series' outdoor sequences. Wander through the historic streets and feel as if you've entered another universe.

A Relaxation and Wellness Retreat Plan

This wellness-focused schedule is ideal for anyone wishing to rest and refresh.

Day 1: Spa Day - Stay in Aqva Gerunda Banys Romans and spend the day relaxing in the hot pools. Book a massage or a facial to complete the pampering experience.

Day 2: Yoga and Meditation - Take a yoga class at Yoga Girona to stretch, breathe, and calm yourself. Spend the afternoon wandering along the River Onyar or exploring the tranquil Sant Daniel Valley.

Day 3: Nature Escape - Enjoy a leisurely trek in the Garrotxa Volcanic Zone Natural Park. The routes are mild, and the view is breathtaking, with lush forests and ancient volcanoes providing a tranquil backdrop.

- In the evening, eat a quiet lunch at El Celler de Can Roca while reflecting on your wellness experience in Girona.

Whether you're a first-time visitor or an experienced Girona traveler, these itineraries have something for everyone. From adventure and relaxation to food and fandom, Girona caters to every type of traveler, regardless of interest or speed. The city's beauty is in its adaptability—and no matter how you choose to experience it, Girona promises to leave you with memories that will stay long after you leave.

Chapter 23

CONCLUSION AND FINAL THOUGHTS

The enchantment of Girona is difficult to capture in words. Whether it's your first visit or your tenth, the city has a way of engulfing you, luring you in with its medieval elegance, lively culture, and the steady hum of daily life that flows down its small alleys. As I sit here, reminiscing on my several visits to this Catalan treasure, I realize that Girona is more than just a beautiful location; it is a sensation, a place that leaves an everlasting stamp on your spirit.

If there's one thing I've learned from my time in Girona, it's that no two visits are the same. The city is continuously changing, but it manages to preserve its rich history and customs in a way that feels both timeless and modern. There's something deeply rewarding about meandering through the Old Town, discovering new nooks of the Jewish Quarter, or coming across an art gallery you hadn't spotted before. Girona never becomes old since there is always more to discover.

So, as you prepare to say goodbye (for the time being), I'd like to take a moment to reflect on what makes Girona so special, offer some final travel recommendations, and wish you a fond farewell—until we meet again.

Reflecting on Girona's Unique Charm

Girona exudes an irresistible charm that strikes you the instant you arrive. It's in the way the Onyar River runs gently through the city, its banks dotted with colorful houses that appear to have been plucked straight from a painting. It's in the intimidating magnificence of the Girona Cathedral, which towers over the city like a quiet sentinel, its steps worn smooth by generations of pilgrims, visitors, and, let's be honest, a few Game of Thrones enthusiasts reenacting events from King's Landing.

The contrasts in Girona are what make it so appealing to me. It's a city where ancient history meets modern living, where you can wander down streets dating back to Roman times while sipping a craft beer at a fashionable pub just across the block. The city's size is part of what makes it so appealing—small enough

210

to feel intimate and manageable while large enough to provide an endless range of experiences, from Michelin-starred dining at El Celler de Can Rocato to quiet moments of introspection in the Sant Daniel valley.

Beyond the sights, it is the people of Girona who provide the city with authentic warmth. The inhabitants are proud of their past while also welcoming newcomers with open arms. I've had several chats in Girona's cafés and markets that began with a simple grin and concluded with me discovering a local's favorite hidden place or being invited to have a glass of vermut. Girona is more than just a destination to visit; it is an experience that will linger with you long after you leave.

Make the Most of Your Time in the City

Whether you have three days or a week to spend in Girona, there are numerous ways to make the most of your stay. The goal is to achieve a balance between seeing the must-see attractions and allowing yourself to explore at your own speed. Trust me when I say that Girona rewards the curious traveler.

One of my favorite ways to begin the day in Girona is to get a coffee and a pastry at a local café—La Fabricais is a terrific choice for this—before venturing out on foot to explore. Girona is a walking city, and some of the best experiences come from simply roaming around and getting lost. The Jewish Quarter is the ideal location for this. Its narrow, twisting alleyways are full of surprises—small courtyards, hidden stairways, and ancient details that you might overlook if you're in a hurry.

Of course, no visit to Girona is complete without a stroll along the Passeig de la Muralla, the medieval walls that provide beautiful views of the city and surrounding countryside. I've walked these walls several times, and each time I'm impressed by how serene and expansive the experience is. There's something about seeing the city from above, watching the Old Town rooftops stretch out before you, that makes you feel both linked to Girona and as if you've stepped into a fairy tale.

Another must-do activity is to spend time beside the Onyar River. The bridges that cross the river provide some of Girona's most famous views, particularly the Pont de les Peixateries Velles (Eiffel Bridge). Don't forget to take a picture of the colorful houses reflected in the water—it's one of those iconic Girona photos that never gets old.

Must-See Spots Before You Leave

On every trip, there comes a point when you realize it's your last day and you stress, thinking of all you still want to do. If you find yourself in this predicament in Girona, don't worry—I've compiled a fast list of must-see places to visit before you depart.

- Girona Cathedral: Even if you've already climbed the steps and explored the interior, it's worth taking a final look. The view of the cathedral from Plaça de la Catedral at sunset is spectacular, and you can sit on the steps and watch as the city is bathed in golden light.

- Jardins dels Alemanys: Tucked away outside the city walls, this park offers a peaceful respite. It's the ideal place to unwind, reflect on your journey, and enjoy a moment of peace before returning home.

- Rocambolesc: If you haven't had ice cream here yet, this is the moment. Jordi Roca's (one of the Roca brothers) masterpieces are both art and dessert, and they're the ideal sweet send-off.

- The Jewish Quarter: One more walk through these ancient lanes is essential. Every time I walk through, I discover something new—a hidden passage, a tiny balcony decked in flowers, or the way the sun hits the stone walls at the perfect angle.

- Plaça de la Independència: This bustling square is ideal for a last lunch or a drink before heading to the airport or train station. Sit outside, order a plate of jamón and olives, and take in the atmosphere one final time.

Final Travel Tips for the Perfect Trip

Before you go, here are some final travel advice to make your trip to Girona pleasant, fun, and memorable:

1. Wear Comfortable Shoes: Girona's cobblestone streets are lovely, but not ideal for high heels. Whether you're exploring the Old Town or trekking the Sant Miqueltrail, a good pair of shoes will save your feet (and mood).

2. Learn a Few Catalan Phrases: While most people in Girona know both Spanish and Catalan, locals love it when visitors try to speak some Catalan. Simply saying "Bon dia" (good morning) or "Gràcies" (thank you) goes a long way.

3. Enjoy the Siesta: Girona, like much of Spain, has a habit of taking a break in the afternoon. Many shops and companies close between 1:30 and 4:30 p.m., so schedule your day appropriately. Use this time to unwind, eat a lengthy lunch, or take a nap—this is the Girona way.

4. Make Reservations in Advance: If you want to eat at one of Girona's top restaurants, such as El Celler de Can Roca, you'll need to make your reservation well in advance. Other popular restaurants, such as Nu Girona or BionBo, still require reservations, particularly on weekends.

5. Take Your Time: Girona is a city best experienced leisurely. Don't try to do too much in one day. Instead, allow the city to unveil itself at its own speed. Sit in a café, linger in a museum, or take an extra walk down the river; you'll be rewarded with deeper experiences.

A Warm Farewell from Girona

As I write this, I imagine you walking through Girona for the last time, soaking in the sights, sounds, and smells of this lovely city. Whether it's the aroma of freshly baked bread wafting from a bakery, the clang of church bells booming through the streets, or the quiet murmur of conversation in a café, Girona has a way of infiltrating your memory and becoming a place you'll never forget.

I have lost track of how many times I've said goodbye to Girona, yet each time feels like a vow to return. The city has that effect—it makes you want more, luring you back with the promise of new discoveries, fresh flavors, and the warmth that only a place steeped in history and culture can provide.

So, as you prepare to depart, I hope you feel the same way. I hope Girona has left an impression on you, just like it did on me. And, whether this is your first trip to Girona or one of many, I am confident that you will remember it long after you return home.

Here is to the next time. Until then, Bon voyage et fins aviat—safe travels, and see you soon.

Chapter 24

USEFUL RESOURCES

When traveling, especially to a city as enthralling as Girona, it's always a good idea to have a few essential materials on hand. Whether you're dealing with a minor travel issue, trying to traverse the Old Town's meandering streets, or impressing the locals with a well-placed Catalan word, this appendix can help. Consider it your Girona survival handbook, complete with practical tools, useful knowledge, and a sprinkle of comedy to keep things light when you need it the most.

I've spent enough time meandering around Girona's historic streets to understand that having the correct materials at your disposal might be the difference between feeling like an intrepid explorer and feeling a little confused. So, here's a list of important contacts, navigational tools, and phrases to help you make the most of your visit in this stunning Catalan city. Let's plunge in!

Emergency Contacts

Nobody wants to think about requiring emergency services while on vacation, but it is always a good idea to be prepared. Girona is a pretty safe city, however if you find yourself in an emergency, here are the main numbers you'll need:

- The emergency number (police, fire, ambulance) is 112.

This is Spain's universal emergency number, so if you need immediate assistance, phone 112. The operators speak several languages, including English, Catalan, and Spanish.

- Local Police (Policia Local): 092.

For non-urgent police problems, please contact Girona's local police. They are kind and have experience assisting travelers. They are available to assist with missing things and small incidents.

- University Hospital of Girona Dr. Josep Trueta

For medical situations, go to Girona's major hospital. Avinguda de França, s/n, 17007 Girona is a fully equipped contemporary hospital with an emergency department.

Phone: +34 972 940 200.

- Pharmacy (Farmàcie)

Pharmacies in Girona are easily identifiable by their green crosses. Many provide 24-hour service and rotate between them. If you're unsure which one is open, visit Farmàcia Francesc Rodríguez at Carrer de l'Argenteria, 7, 17004 Girona.

Phone number: +34 972 214 112.

- Tourist Information Center.

If you require assistance or guidance during your visit, the Girona Tourist Office is an excellent resource. Located in Rambla de la Llibertat 1, they can help with anything from directions to tour recommendations.

Phone: +34 972 010 001.

Website: www.girona.cat/turisme.

Maps and Navigation Tools

Navigating Girona can be simple if you have the appropriate tools. The Old Town's twisting streets can feel like a maze at times, but it all adds to the city's charm. To make things easier, here are some helpful maps and navigational tools:

- Google Maps.

This is the classic way to get about. Whether you're looking for the quickest route to Girona Cathedral or checking out a new eatery, Google Maps will direct you with precision. It also offers walking, driving, and public transportation routes.

Website: www.google.com/maps.

- Map.me

If you prefer offline navigation (because, let's be honest, that overseas data plan might be tricky at times), Maps.me is an excellent choice. You can download Girona's maps to your phone and utilize them offline.

Website: www.maps.me.

- City Mapper

Citymapper comes in handy when using Girona's public transportation. It offers real-time bus schedules, pedestrian routes, and bicycle pathways. The software is straightforward to use, and I found it particularly useful for moving between Girona and the other Costa Brava cities.

Website: www.citymapper.com.

– Komoot

If you're planning a trek or a cycling route (because, let's be honest, Girona is a cyclist's paradise), Komoot is the app for you. This app is ideal for recording outdoor activities and offers a variety of routes in and around Girona, including moderate riverside walks and challenging climbs to Montjuïc Castle.

Website address: www.komoot.com.

Additional Reading and References

Girona's rich history and vibrant culture will entice you to learn more about the city. Here are some recommended reads and websites to help you better understand this intriguing location.

- "The Jews of Girona" written by Anna Fàbrega i Escatllar

This book gives a detailed overview of Girona's Jewish community, which thrived during the medieval period. If you're planning a visit to the Museum of Jewish History, this is an excellent companion book.

- "Catalonia: A Cultural History" by Michael Eaude.

This book provides an instructive and fascinating overview of Catalonia's history and culture. It discusses Girona's importance in the broader Catalan setting and delves into the region's art, architecture, and traditions.

- Girona Tourism Blog.

The Girona Tourism Board's blog is routinely updated with events, hidden gems, and travel recommendations. It's an excellent resource for staying up to date on what's going on in the city while you're visiting.

URL: www.girona.cat/turisme/eng/blog.php.

- "The Shadow of the Wind" by Carlos Ruiz Zafón.

Although this novel is set in Barcelona, it captures the mystical, romantic vibe of Spain's old cities, making it an ideal read for a leisurely afternoon in Girona. Sit in one of the plazas with a coffee and immerse yourself in this fascinating tale of books, secrets, and history.

Useful Local Phrases

Although many people in Girona understand English, knowing a few important words in Catalan (and Spanish) will be quite beneficial. The locals appreciate your efforts, and you'll most likely be greeted with a warm smile for trying. Here are a few Catalan phrases to get you started:

- Bon dia– Good morning

- Bona tarda– Good afternoon

- Bona nit– Good night

- Si us plau– Please

- Gràcies– Thank you

- Perdó– Excuse me / Sorry

- Com estàs?– How are you?

- Quin preu té?– How much does this cost?

- On és…?– Where is…?

- No ho entenc– I don't understand

And just in case you get mixed up, here are the Spanish equivalents:

- Buenos días– Good morning

- Buenas tardes– Good afternoon

- Buenas noches– Good night

- Por favor– Please

- Gracias– Thank you

- Perdón– Excuse me / Sorry

- ¿Cómo estás?– How are you?

- ¿Cuánto cuesta?– How much does this cost?

- ¿Dónde está…?– Where is…?

- No entiendo– I don't understand

Tip: If in doubt, start with a simple Bon Dia. Even if they respond in Spanish or English, most Gironians smile.

Glossary

Traveling to Girona will surely introduce you to new terminology, names, and dishes. Here's a glossary of crucial words you'll hear during your stay, so you can feel like a local from the start:

- Barri Vell, Girona's Old Town, is noted for its medieval streets and historic structures.

- Passeig de la Muralla: A path that runs along Girona's ancient city walls and provides panoramic views of the city.

- Plaça de la Independència- A bustling square in Girona with cafés and restaurants ideal for people-watching.

Call- The Jewish Quarter of Girona, one of Europe's best-preserved.

- Tapas are little cuisine dishes that are often served as snacks or appetizers throughout Spain. They are a must-try!

Calçots are a sort of green onion grilled and eaten with romesco sauce, which is a Catalan delicacy, especially in the spring.

- Cava, Catalonia's famous sparkling wine, is commonly served with tapas or on special occasions.

- Romesco is a rich, nutty sauce created with roasted peppers, almonds, and garlic. It tastes great with seafood, veggies, and grilled meats.

- Mató- A fresh Catalan cheese that is traditionally served with honey for dessert.

With these materials, you'll be able to travel Girona with ease. Whether you're taking in the sights, meeting locals, or sampling the city's gastronomic delights, this guide will make your vacation easier, richer, and more pleasurable. Girona is a city that is both welcoming and attractive, and I am confident that you will leave with lifelong memories. Safe travels, and I hope to see you soon on those wonderful streets!

Addresses and Locations for Popular Accommodation

When vacationing in Girona, you want a hotel that not only provides comfort but also adds to the allure of the experience. The beauty of Girona's accommodations is that they cater to a wide range of preferences, from luxury seekers to those who want a quaint, boutique atmosphere.

- Hotel Nord 1901 Superior.

Hotel Nord 1901, located in the heart of Girona, is a boutique hotel that mixes modern conveniences with Catalan architecture's timeless elegance. With its simple design, rooftop patio, and pool, it's the ideal combination of comfort and sophistication. It's only a short walk from Girona Cathedral and Plaça de la Independència, making it an excellent base for exploring the city.

Address: Carrer Nord 7-9, 17001 Girona.

Website: www.nord1901.com.

Hotel Ciutat de Girona.

If you're looking for a modern hotel in the heart of Girona, Hotel Ciutat de Gironahas certainly you covered. This hotel near the Pont de Pedra features elegant rooms and a heated indoor pool. The area is busy but not overcrowded, and you're only a short walk from the Onyar River and Rambla de la Llibertat.

Address: Carrer Nord 2, 17001 Girona.

- Hotel Historic

Hotel Historic is a must-visit for those looking to immerse themselves in history. This lovely hotel, located in the Old Town and just steps from the Girona Cathedral, features rooms with exposed stone walls, wooden beams, and antique furnishings. It's the type of setting where you can nearly sense the centuries of history surrounding you while still enjoying modern amenities.

Address: Carrer Bellmirall 4A, 17004 Girona.

Website address: www.hotelhistoric.com.

Addresses and Locations of Popular Restaurants and Cafés

Girona is a food lover's dream, with some fantastic eating options ranging from Michelin-starred restaurants to tiny cafés ideal for people watching.

El Celler de Can Roca

El Celler de Can Roca is a must-visit restaurant in Girona. The Roca brothers own this three-Michelin-starred restaurant, which is frequently recognized as one of the greatest in the world. The tasting menu is a work of art, with dishes that challenge traditional Catalan cuisine. Make sure to book well in advance, as tables here are in hot demand.

Address: Carrer Can Sunyer 48, 17007 Girona

Website: www.cellercanroca.com.

- Bion Bo.

BionBois is the ideal destination for those seeking something more intimate but equally spectacular. This restaurant serves a tasting menu that emphasizes seasonal, local ingredients, and the dishes are designed with an artistic flair. It's a little off the main route, but it's well worth visiting for its innovative take on modern Catalan cuisine.

Address: Carrer de la Creu 10, 17002 Girona

La Fabrica Girona

La Fabrica Girona is a must-see for bicycle enthusiasts or anyone looking for a wonderful brunch place. Christian Meier, an ex-professional cyclist, and his wife manage this café in the Old Town, which is popular with both locals and tourists. The coffee is delicious, and the avocado toast is legendary. It's the ideal place to refuel before a day of exploration.

Address: Carrer de la Llebre 3, 17004 Girona.

- Rocambolesc Gelateria.

For a sweet treat, visit Rocambolesc, the fanciful ice cream shop owned by Jordi Roca, the pastry chef from El Celler de Can Roca. The inventive ice cream flavors are as distinct as you'd imagine, and the packaging is right out of a storybook. The warm brioche ice cream sandwich is a must try!

Address: Carrer de Santa Clara 50, 17001 Girona.

Website address: www.rocambolesc.com.

Addresses and Locations of Popular Bars and Clubs

After a day of visiting Girona's rich history, you might want to relax with a drink (or several) at one of the city's lively bars or clubs. Girona's nightlife caters to all tastes, whether you like handmade cocktails or a raucous night out.

- Siddhartha Lounge Bar

Looking for something more laid-back? Siddharta Lounge Bar is the place to be. It's the ideal place to unwind with friends, thanks to its laid-back environment, comfortable seating, and extensive beverage menu. Furthermore, their outdoor terrace has a magnificent view of the Old Town, making it an ideal spot for an evening drink.

Address: Carrer de la Barca 10, 17004 Girona

– Sunset Jazz Club

Sunset Jazz Club is Girona's premier live jazz venue, offering a night of beautiful sounds and a refined environment. It's a quiet, private spot in the Old Town with an excellent drink menu. If you're lucky, you might catch a local jazz quartet performing songs that create the ideal atmosphere for a relaxing evening.

Address: Carrer Jaume Pons Martí, 12, 17001 Girona.

- The Lapsus Cafe

If you're looking for a more dynamic and active night out, Lapsus Café is an excellent choice. This modern pub is popular among locals and boasts a lively, entertaining ambiance. With a wonderful range of cocktails and music that will have you on your feet, it's the ideal spot to dance the night away.

Address: Carrer Ciutadans 9, 17004 Girona

Addresses and Locations of the Top Attractions

Girona's rich history, architecture, and culture are on full show in its numerous attractions. Here are the must-see attractions that should be on everyone's itinerary.

- Girona Cathedral

The majestic Girona Cathedral dominates the city skyline, and for good reason. The great staircase and breathtaking Gothic architecture are not to be missed.

Make sure to go inside to witness the famed Tapestry of Creation and climb the bell tower for spectacular views of the city.

Address: Plaça de la Catedral, S/N, 17004 Girona.

Website address: www.catedraldegirona.cat.

Passeig de la Muralla

A hike along the Passeig de la Muralla offers panoramic views of Girona and the surrounding countryside. These historic walls enclose the Old Town and provide some of the best views in the city. It's a relaxing walk that also gives you a good sense of Girona's history.

Entrance: Several entry points throughout the Old Town

– Museum of Jewish History

This museum, located in the heart of Girona's Jewish Quarter, offers an in-depth look into the city's Middle Ages Jewish history. It is one of Europe's best-preserved Jewish districts, and the museum itself is a peaceful, reflective area rich with history.

Address: Carrer de la Força 8, 17004 Girona

URL: www.girona.cat/call/eng.

- Arabic Baths

The Arab Baths, located in the Old Town, are an excellent example of medieval architecture combining Romanesque and Moorish influences. While no longer in use, the baths provide an intriguing peek into Girona's past, and their tranquil setting makes for a pleasant, brief visit.

Address: Carrer Ferran el Catòlic, S/N, 17004 Girona.

Website address: www.banysarabs.org.

Plaça de la Independència

Plaça de la Independència, one of Girona's most bustling squares, is crowded with cafés, restaurants, and pubs. It's a fantastic area to sit and enjoy a coffee or drink while watching the world go by. It's also an excellent starting point for exploring the city center's shops and streets.

Address: Plaza de la Independència, 17001 Girona.

Girona is a city that seamlessly combines its ancient roots with a modern, vibrant culture, as evidenced by the diverse range of lodgings, culinary options, nightlife, and attractions. Whether you're roaming the old medieval alleyways, enjoying in delicious meals, or sipping cocktails at jazz bars, Girona has a memorable experience around every corner. Bring your map, appetite, and curiosity—you will not be disappointed!

Printed in Great Britain
by Amazon

57903011R00136